Manchild Dying in the Promised Land
Strategies to Save Black Males

Sallie M. Cuffee, Ph.D.

African American Images

DEDICATION

To my nephews and those beloved ones who adopted me as their Aunt. Their fight for life's infinite possibilities drove me to write this book.

Carlos, Sr., Glenn, Jr., Rudolph, Jr., David, Jr., Sean, Crist, Cedric, Jr., Rashad, DeShawn, Adrain and Yaureibo

To the boys of the Long Ridge Community who died too young or languish in an imprisoned state.

To the faculty at Medgar Evers College/City University of New York, salvaging lives and strengthening tomorrows.

First Edition, First Printing

Front cover illustration by Harold Carr, Jr.

Copyright © 2008 by Dr. Sallie M. Cuffee, Ph.D.

Printed in the United States of America

10-Digit ISBN #: 1-934155-13-6

13-Digit ISBN #: 978-1-934155-13-4

ACKNOWLEDGMENT

I want to acknowledge my thanks and appreciation to my family for their generous support and commitment to me and whom without, this project would not have been possible. My mother, Mrs. Daisy Cuffee; my sisters, Janet R. Cuffee, Priscilla I. Cuffee, Mrs. Selena Cuffee-Glenn and her husband, Keith, my brother, Mr. Rudolph Crist Cuffee, Sr. and his wife, Kim, and nephew, Carlos Brown and his wife, Tamara. To my colleagues at Medgar Evers College: Professor Amir Al-Islam for his unflinching support throughout this project, for the lively discussions with Professor Thomas Edwards to Dr. Scharlene Snowden who read the entire manuscript. To my wonderful family at Spoonbread Restaurant in Harlem: Kenny, Arlene, Demetrius, Deborah, Lois, and Desiree. To the wonderful support staff at Medgar Evers College: Ms. Wenda Delpesche, Ms. Rhonda Williams, Ms. Pauline Canady, Ms. Samantha Gregoire-James, and Mr. Akeem: IT extraordinaire Andrew Jackson; and the fine library staff, Mr. William Daly and Alexis Oulanov.

FOREWORD

I was moved by Dr. Sallie Cuffee's passion and sincerity in *Manchild Dying in the Promised Land*. Her book is one follow-up to the powerful classic by the late Claude Brown, *Manchild in the Promise Land*. What happened to our males? I would like for all of you to observe African American boys in kindergarten and then contrast that with a visit of our males in 9th grade. What happened to their innocence, joy, enthusiasm and their dreams? These questions and more are raised in this book. Cuffee leaves no area unscathed, schools, homes, churches, communities, politicians, criminal justice system and businesses are all dissected. Has crack been more devastating on the Black community than slavery? Is the future of African people in the hands of single parent mothers because so many African American males have become sperm donors? What is the relationship between special education and prison? Illiteracy and incarceration? Ritalin and crack? What percent of the problems and solutions are internal? What percent of the above is external? Cuffee gives an excellent analysis. I encourage you to read this book if you are concerned about the future of African American males.

Jawanza Kunjufu author of *Raising Black Boys*

CONTENTS

**The Black Youth's Burden: Violence,
Death and Incarceration**

**Where Do We Go From Here:
Community "Bootstrap" Strategies**

INTRODUCTION

Who Will Save the Young Black Male?
We Who Believe in Freedom

To be an Afro-American, or an American black, is to be in the situation, intolerably exaggerated, of all those who have ever found themselves part of a civilization which they could in no wise honorably defend—which they were compelled, indeed, endlessly to attack and condemn—and who yet spoke out of the most passionate love, hoping to make the kingdom new, to make it honorable and worthy of life.

James Baldwin

Until the killing of Black men, the Black mothers' sons, becomes as important to the rest of the country as a white mother's son, we who believe in freedom will not rest until it comes.

Ella Baker, SCLC's Executive Director

Young black males suffer from being expendable casualties of a heartless Katrina-like political climate in this nation, where, in both cases, there is little mercy—let alone money—for society's neediest. In the case of these young black males, with record high school dropout, escalating unemployment, and epidemic incarceration, they are worse off than ever before. "Manchildren" is what author Claude Brown's chilling memoirs christened this endangered teen population decades ago. For these social crises and more, manchildren are being blamed as the root cause of their own traumatic conditions, even as they are ill-equipped to address their deep-rooted, multi-tentacled problems in any systematic way. Lest we forget, they are children—America's forgotten children, too—and are desperately in need of substantial government intervention into their dire circumstances. But because they are poor, black males and young, they have been written off the national agenda and left to the clutches of a menacing and racist societal system, bent upon exacerbating their crisis conditions and ensuring their disposability in America's twenty-first century global future.

Subsequently, throughout this book I argue that the life-threatening trials of young black males do not unfold and operate in social isolation. Their present crisis conditions are adversely linked to the socioeconomic priorities driving this nation's political life. Without prioritizing the necessary resources for some of society's most vulnerable, such as young black males, epidemic conditions are severely aggravating their social status as disposable. Starting with an over 50 percent dropout rate in urban schools among minority children guarantees their candidacy for unemployment, poverty, and prison.[1] Unregulated handguns proliferate in their troubled neighborhoods, anxious to fall into juvenile hands. The intensification of drug wars due to economic downsizing or urban job flight triggers perilous risk conditions for gang activity, homicide and/or prison. Racial profiling breeds a dangerous suspicion of those many who may be innocent with tragic blood-letting consequence. In the case of the executed Sean Bell[2] and his injured friends, the verdict of acquittal by Justice Arthur Cooperman nods visible assent to the escalation of this practice of open-season slaughter on young black males, with the justice system's tacit collusion. What the verdict declared unequivocally is that being innocent means absolutely nothing when "his sin is black skin."[3] And it is that very "fifty bullets-type" perverse perception which drives racial profiling with a vengeance, resulting in young black male detainment and usual arrest. (Now with the courts' outright license and complicity, more young black males will suffer the unrighteous fate of Sean Bell, an NYPD lynching on principle; for the vigilante officers killed Bell because they could.[4] They believed that they were above the law.) Without any modest effort at subterfuge, no longer cloak-and-dagger hidden, but now, out front and in the unafraid open poses an insidious example of the mechanisms of institutional racism at work, much facilitated by powerful societal decision-makers like a New York Supreme Court Justice, who hold and control the unacknowledged reins to the manchild's predestined life and death fate. His guilt or innocence matters little; the manchild's future is already forfeited— and this is no exaggerated understatement, to be bluntly honest. Besieged with such a lethal combination of trials-by-fire, without question, turns young black males into ideal candidates for incarceration, criminalization and homicide, jeopardizing a whole generation of manchildren whose lives are placed at high-alert risk.

Whether the black community chooses to admit it or not, at some moral level, society is complicit with social systems that are militantly anti-young black males and repressive of manchildren's life chances. In all actuality, the attack upon manchildren's civil liberties, as seen in Bell's unjustified homicide,[5] for instance, was just another warning sign of the sea change in America's post-sixties' civil rights politics. And through such grisly realities as a Bell murder, citizens are crudely reminded that this is really an attack upon every American's civil liberties. It portends the growing reality of what it means to live in an encroaching police state,[6] seen especially in the National Security Agency's spying on American citizens without warrants and the erosion of civil liberties, consented in the disregard of protecting individuals from government intrusion. Equal protection under the law is up for grabs in just about every community whether American citizens admit or not. Though most evident in vulnerable black, immigrant[7] and Hispanic communities, but in time, no community can be disenfranchised without disadvantaging the nation as a whole.

Though manchildren are overly maligned by the public rhetoric as "super-predators" or the cause of "crime being out of control" and marched off to jail cells as a perverse solution to young black male existence, the threatening conditions of criminalization, death and disposability they face on a daily basis are not solely the gratuitous labor of their own hands. Sure, some responsibility belongs to them. But in saying that, at the same time, I strongly assert that manchildren are more of a victim than has heretofore been acknowledged of that ruthless social matrix which justifies their untimely deaths, profiles them for criminalization, and sponsors the continuation of life-defeating conditions through public policy decisions.

To be sure, in their case, ill-advised public policies have produced an unprecedented amount of misery for the black community in this forfeiture of young lives. This leads to one of the problematic aspects that manchildren face in attaining social justice in this liberal democracy; that is, public policies or laws are written and enforced with the assumption that manchildren have unlimited choices, only they make bad choices or the choices they make are wrong. The liberal dogma of equal opportunity and access, no matter how illusionary, insists that all U.S. citizens spring from the same zero-sum reality to succeed, all free to choose from unlimited choices. The playing field is allegedly equal, in other words. Yet, that is the furthest from the truth in the life experience of young black males. Although declared accessible to all, liberal constitutional rights and privileges, choices for the purpose of this exercise, have always been selectively conferred when race is regarded as a factor, even in a post-civil rights America. Bell, for instance, couldn't even secure equal protection under the law. What happens, in the case of the criminal justice system, with racial bias rampant in law enforcement and sentencing, is that manchildren are singled out to be indiscriminately punished by an appallingly unfair and unequal system of justice. As this introduction will bear out, this is just one hostile institution, albeit central, penalizing manchildren for being born poor, black, and male in America's unpromised land.

Then, in truth, what are the choices manchildren truly possess?

Free But Not Equal

Manchildren of today recognize that they might be legally free but wretchedly unequal in this democratic society. Perhaps, not far in circumstances from Frantz Fanon's wretched of the earth, but surely they are America's truly disinherited. When it comes to their life chances, the American world that manchildren inhabit is deterministically flawed as choiceless. And this errant state of existence does not pretend to endow them with their rightful due: a status of social equality secured with the guarantees of life, liberty and the pursuit of happiness. Keenly aware of the beleaguered status of manchildren, hip hop author and powerful advocate Kevin Powell, in his popular book, *Who's Gonna Take the Weight,* weighs in a moral defense on behalf of those counted, in his own words, as "socially dead." As one who speaks from the humble platform of his own ghetto kinship with manchildren, his protest is that manchildren are being denied real choices in an unequal America. In his eyes, they are being barred from the freedoms which liberalism most proudly touts because of America's original "sin" of racism, grafted on to black skin, which refuses them the promises and privileges endowed the other America by birth. Powell disparages the fact that most times manchildren's hollow choices lie somewhere between two soulless evils: prison or death. From all accounts, manchildren are being crushed, brutally so, by the perversion of the American dream; its worst nightmare is what they endure. Thus, liberal notions of freedom and choice, of equal rights, are becoming severely problematic for young black males in an unequal nation that has shredded much of its social safety net and taken on a new national priority—security—at the expense of other pressing social priorities in a post-September 11 world.

Wanting to cement his argument in the ghetto "concrete," Powell resurrects Tupac Shakur, that controversial personality, as a young black male who had to face the demons of ghetto life and triumph over formidable odds stacked against him, as it is for every manchild born in a "concrete jungle" reality. Powell writes:

"Well, Tupac had choices" or "Tupac knew what he was getting himself into." What choices, really, did Tupac have? He was born poor, so he knew he had to survive. While middle-class White and Black children have the option of thinking about what they want to do with their lives, Tupac decided early on that being a rapper was his surest and perhaps only ticket out of the ghetto…. That does not suggest choice; it suggests doing what you have to do to survive in the ghetto world that produced you.[8]

Tupac, in fact, portrayed his own life in these thorny words: "The rose that grew from a crack in the concrete/ proving nature's law wrong it learned 2 walk without having feet."[9] Intuitively, manchildren sense the forbidden odds they are up against, living the socially uncircumcised life of society's castaways. For Shakur, his ghetto birth inaugurated an adolescence of ill-fated trials that seemingly doomed him long before he met his violent demise in the intersection of Flamingo Road and Koval Lane in Las Vegas, as the tragic victim of a gang-style shootout. Notwithstanding, Powell's provocative reading of Tupac's limited life choices fiercely interrogates the institutional matrix that condemns manchildren long before their lives begin, and ultimately detonates them as "walking time bombs."

So what are the choices, as Powell defiantly queries, chiding this liberal farce of equal opportunity and access, if a manchild's life chances are already ensnared in a crippling web of "nurture" social impediments? Absentee fathers at a national high in the black community, the product of inferior school systems, corralled in an environment that suffers from all the ills of urban blight, profiled every day of his life, and the crippling job downsizing in a technocratic economy, how much of the blame can he bear for his severely aborted life choices and to what extent is his personal accountability? Where is the institutional responsibility?

Moralizing by a more conservative wing preaches the lack of personal responsibility to scourge manchildren for supposedly squandering their life chances. I contend that this is simply one more ideological ploy to conceal society's willful theft of them. What's at stake here is that the liberal assumption of the manchild being a free agent with unlimited choices excuses the way in which institutions are left blameless for the fresh blood on their own hands in young black males' death and demise.

Introduction

Without a doubt, America's moral and political traditions have never quite come to grips with that complicated legacy of African slavery and its lethal consequences for later generations of African Americans. Even with historical periods of race relations liberalization, black people's personal and bodily realities have been persistently crushed by the supposedly superior claims of liberal "progress" and its unflinching pledge to the protection of white majority rule, mystified in civil liberties language like freedom, democracy, and individual rights.[10] For that trampled manchild and his blood community, arguably the liabilities of a choiceless world dog their steps and weigh heavily against one of the most cherished of human yearnings, that is, to be free, equal, and self-determined.

But Powell's indictment of that liberal notion of free and equal does force a serious interrogation of that at-large question: What about the structural practices of white racism?[11] Are they perceived as neutral factors in the high incidence of young black male death and demise as well as incarceration? On the contrary, my intent is to argue persistently throughout this book that, with unmitigated force, such structural practices of racism have operated with genocidal consequences to breach the life chances of this generation of manchildren, as it has historically in truncating the national life of the black community.

"Savage Inequalities"

Highly respected sociologist Andrew Hacker in his classic text, *Two Nations: Black and White, Separate, Hostile, Unequal,* after the findings of the 1960's Kerner Commission Report,[12] documents what is still appallingly apparent: that decades later, conditions impaling black life signal a bitter truth about the intransigent nature of racism in America. So pervasive in endangering young black males' life chances, Hacker queries whether there is an "understated strategy" of annihilation complicit in creating the choiceless world to which manchildren are consigned and in which they anticipate their premature death and demise.[14] In considering this section, I borrow aptly from the convictions of educator and activist Jonathan Kozol, who denounces our nation's social neglect of school children as "savage inequalities." Such describe in selective detail, some of the insidious social and institutional mechanisms of annihilation at work in theft of young black males' life chances. What becomes evident is that "savage inequalities" early catapult manchildren into the punitive estrangement of a choiceless world. In the urban wildernesses where manchildren traverse and beyond those blighted borders, various social and institutional mechanisms are more than willing to intensify patterns of isolationism and alienation made injurious to their tenuous existence. Many such patterns are obvious; others less so. As a result, less often do manchildren navigate successfully the forces that determine much of their failure in life, whether it's dropping out of school or being preyed upon by law enforcement personnel. In their failures, they simply believe that they acted alone as a result of personal choice, and thus, they are solely to blame. "It's their individual failing," is how it's moralized in the American media, adding fuel to an already full-blown antagonistic flame. In focusing upon the "understated" forces of annihilation operating in their lives— often with vengeful consequences—this book seeks to provide a candid analysis of such crime conditions that may yield these manchildren, their families, and the black community fresh insight into just how deeply at-risk their lives really are.

Only the most ruthless enemy in today's society against manchildren's freedom is the criminal justice system. It is one monumental social and political entity that is able to coerce and contain their future. Playing a decisive role in multiplying young black males' social disadvantages, the judicial system acts in concert with other bureaucratic entities to funnel young black males out of their respective local contexts, most times urban, into the criminal justice system. To be crystal clear here: "The cradle-to-prison superhighway (CPS) is a network of legislation, policy, practice, and structural racism that has fostered blacks being incarcerated at unconscionable levels at increasingly younger ages for increasingly minor acts," writes James Bell of *The Covenant*.[15] This emerging CPS network serves as an important conduit in the well-oiled wheels of the prison industrial complex.[16] Rendering ever true, manchildren's lives acquire distinct currency in the economy of prisonization. Documenting this fact first-hand, public policy analyst John Flateau of the Dubois Bunche Center, in his study of the operation of the prison industrial complex in Brooklyn, New York, confirms that young black males are systematically targeted and criminalized.[17] The vulnerability of their life plight is not unique to Brooklyn, though. Black male youth are profiled as the nation's worst crime problem, to which political solutions invariably involve the criminal justice system.[18]

Moreover, institutional racism is never more evident than in the biased sentencing process that functions as a two-track system at work in the criminal justice system. For instance, after entering the judicial system, white and black juveniles with the same criminal records are treated in radically different ways. Historian and African American research scholar Manning Marable cites recent Justice Department statistics corroborating the rampant unequal treatment black youth endure as a matter of due process.

> Among white youth offenders, 66 percent are referred to juvenile courts, while only 31 percent of the African-American youth are taken there. Blacks make up 44 percent of those detained in juvenile jails, 46 percent of all those tried in adult criminal courts, as well as 58 percent of all juveniles who are warehoused in prisons.[19]

What's more, this disparity is ever more pronounced in the sentencing guidelines for powder and crack cocaine. "About 90 percent of crack arrests are of African Americans and Hispanics, while 75 percent of powder cocaine arrests are of whites. Under federal law, it takes only five grams of crack cocaine to trigger a five-year mandatory minimum sentence. It takes 500 grams of powder cocaine to get this same sentence."[20] The message is lethally clear: black life is cheaper than white. Sent to jail for a lesser crime returns black boys and men to chattel-like statuses. Laden on to manchildren's already burdensome disadvantage is their frustration with how the justice system arbitrarily dishes out punishment. To date, these disproportionate sentencing laws continue to funnel black youth and men at epidemic numbers into the pipelines of the prison industrial complex. Increasingly this form of social entrapment awaits the lives of countless number of young black males.

Transferring black youth to adult court for prosecution on a daily basis, furthermore, is symbolic of how the system throws up its hand and gives up on black youth. In New York City, "youth in the age category 16-20 years are treated as adults for the purpose of criminal prosecution."[21] Imprisonment, once reserved for hardened adult criminals, has become the catch-all response to black youth delinquency. Choosing a criminal solution, when it comes to young black males, to solve problems that are actually the result of deep-seated socioeconomic ills has only served to escalate the numbers being criminalized and incarcerated. Now, more than ever, manchildren desperately need early detection and intervention into their hard lives through effective school and afterschool programs, tutorial assistance, psychological help when signs of maladjustment are visible, extracurricular activities at more community's Boys and Girls Clubs, job training programs to set urban youth upon the straight and narrow of becoming productive citizens of society, and just generally a solid national investment in the treatment needs of at-risk youth. Instead, imprisonment is politicized as the most effective form of intervention.

From these dire criminal justice statistics, some of the black community's worst fears are confirmed; that is, our youth are headed toward becoming a lost generation. With few institutional buffers to salvage their disposable lives, a rite of passage for young black male teens growing up today will be their unavoidable contact with the criminal justice system. The Sentencing Project, a nonprofit advocacy group based in Washington, D.C., which conducts studies of criminal justice biases and advocates for sentencing reform, confirms these suspicions and issues this dire prediction: "For this generation of black children today, there's almost an inevitable prospect of going to prison."[22]

What other crushing blows of disposability are aimed at manchildren on a daily basis? Early in their lives, black males are casualties of the school systems' lowered expectations. Psychologist Jawanza Kunjufu, a premiere educational consultant on black males and specialist in devising educational strategies to counter any prospective "conspiracy" against black boys, counsels that this assault upon the manchild's academic self-esteem harms him as early as the fourth grade.[23] School dropout rates are symptomatic of the problem. "In schools with minority students as the majority, only 50.2% actually graduate."[24] Of that young black male population in prison, middle-and high-school dropouts are disproportionately overrepresented.[25] It's a short leap to projecting that black youth who drop out of school incur a greater risk of being unemployed, and are likely to participate in gang activity and/or go to prison. Already they are casualties before they can grasp the questionable bootstraps of opportunity. Serving a life sentence in a maximum-security prison, one gang banger recalls, "My sixth-grade graduation was my first and last. Actually, it was the last time I ever seriously attended school—for academic purposes."[26] Because of severely limited resources, with an eroded tax base, school systems in poor neighborhoods perform under a huge handicap that portends lasting consequences for black children. Unable to offer the range of services required to salvage black youth, schools underserve black children, and in short, end up failing them.[27]

The 2001 "No Child Left Behind" (NCLB) Act, intended as a presidential panacea for the nation's neediest schools and children, has done little better in fixing the failed school problem. Since its passage in 2001 by the Bush

administration, one of the major criticisms repeated is that the law underfunds innovative curriculum and teacher development solutions that are designed to bring students up to par—an essential help for black and Hispanic students who often play catch-up—while waving a big stick of "externally imposed 'accountability' standards."[28] Drawing from the research compiled in the article, "Taming the Beast," Dierdre G. Paul cites the thorny problem in these words: "To expect schools to wipe out long-standing academic achievement gaps while denying them substantial new resources...is not an 'accountability' system."[29] Few would disagree that the NCLB has suffered from an overkill of rhetoric without the necessary presidential political will to ensure that educational resources get to the country's neediest children. In one of its more contentious features, its mandatory testing shows just how far these children have been left behind. For forgotten black and brown children, this bad faith Act dramatizes the "too little, too late" investment in ensuring their future and demonstrates how under prioritized black children's academic survival is in this nation. More than noble-sounding presidential rhetoric, urban schools need rehabilitation with competitive curricula, revamped with certified/qualified teachers, innovative models of public education to meet specific population needs, and indeed monies for support services targeted for early intervention to avoid academic failure. Shore up the academic infrastructure, I say to extend black and brown manchildren's short-circuited lives. On the contrary, this nation's investment in this generation of manchildren has only been to exacerbate their criminalization.

On any given day, one of every 14 black children has a parent who is shackled in bondage to the new global plantation—simply put, prisons. The catastrophic impact of mass incarceration on the black family is being weighed on the same horrendous scales as slavery. The black family is being disrupted and left destitute in such vital ways that it begs the question whether it has the resilience to fully recover from such formidable odds to secure a future. Definitely, there is a crisis in the village. Threatened with family separation, weakening parental bonds, the lack of social stability, economic displacement, and political disenfranchisement finds a perverse nexus in incarceration, preying relentlessly upon the meager soul, economic, and social resources of the black community. In all of this, black children are the most vulnerable, suffering some of the greatest impediments due to the parental incarcerated state, and are the unheard, invisible victims.[30] With such devastating losses in human capital, much unfathomable, mass incarceration might be the worst case scenario facing the black community since slavery.[31] Thus, the present state of mass incarceration in the black community is not to be understood solely in individual or personal responsibility terms, but seen as a systematic attack upon the black family, upon black children, and ultimately, upon the future survival of the black community itself. And, of course, not by happenstance are the conditions of exploitation and disempowerment of the black community allowed to prevail.[32] The estranged, crisis conditions undermining the black community's survival, linked to the criminalization and incarceration of a race, is beyond "meting out individual punishment for individual crimes,"[33] but practiced as the current national policy of the U.S. government. It accomplishes no other end than the rounding up of a race for disposability.

What other staggering conditions account for that inflated morbidity found among young black males? For nearly the past 30 years, firearm homicides have headed the list as the leading cause of death among young African American males. Much of this ruthless slaughter in the black community can be traced to the ample supply of unregulated handguns, supplying the fire power of black teen death. Between the ages of 15-24, black males were almost five times more likely to be injured by firearms than white males in the same age group. Black "teens are killing each other for some stupid things like chains, drugs, money, girlfriend or boyfriend or for just a stupid argument," grieves one teenager about the crisis. In a recent news flash in Suffolk, Virginia, a fourteen-year old assailant sped away from the gunfire scene on a ten-speed bicycle. What would turn adolescent children into killers? Readily available handguns litter city streets, have turned neighborhoods into combat zones. Who would dare to disagree that unregulated handguns have escalated this surge of juvenile murders? Often these youthful offenders are close friends and casual acquaintances of their victims. Kenneth Rankin, 17-year old, while busy enjoying a dice game with his pal, 16-year old Sam Gray, got into an argument that sparked a violent altercation, leading to Kenneth being shot in the head.[34] Marian Wright Edelman, founder and longtime president of the Children's Defense Fund, protests this unregulated gun violence as the "slaughter of children."

Worsening the social odds against manchildren, suicide emerges as a silent killer stalking the youth of the black community, and has evolved as one of those unprecedented destructive forces in black male teen life. "Teenage males account for a huge portion of that increase, with the suicide rate for Black males between the ages of 15-19 rising an astronomical 146 percent, eight times higher than the rate for their White counterparts."[35] A once long-held belief, "black folks don't commit suicide," is belied by its rise among young black men, and figures as another deadly factor coalescing to abort black children's short-lived lives. The increase in the suicide rate among black male youth shows that they are not expressing the "madd" love for themselves as many are fond of proclaiming, but are anxiously ready to brave the fires of finality (death) as a quick retreat from life's morbid pain.

Suicide is the third leading cause of death among black youth ages 15-19 years old, according to statistics compiled by the Center for Disease Control and Prevention. Young black males experienced the largest increase within that age group. A 2000 report put out by the *Philadelphia Tribune* estimates a startling 500,000 African-American teens will attempt suicide.[36] What has sparked this silent epidemic among young black males is yet to be fully determined. Research associate Sean Joe, at the Center for Study of Youth Policy at University of

Introduction

Pennsylvania's School of Social Work, calls attention to the fact that young black males suffer from an extreme dislike from others in our society.

> We stress "leave no child behind," but as soon as they become youth and young adults we criticize and demonize them.... We call them super predators and wild wolf packs. What that does is create a social and cultural index that makes them think "I'm on my own. There's no one out there for me," so it conditions their attitude and their life expectancy.[37]

Even worse, on the part of some male teens, ritualizing a gun culture with a "shoot-or-be-shot" attitude endemic to tough street, and then susceptible to anxieties which afflict all teens, handicap them in critical ways that many manchildren find it difficult to cope and consequently choose a deathly alternative like suicide as their permanent solution from living. Just as disturbing, many have also adopted a "ready to die" attitude. With life expectancy low and mainstream economic opportunities in short supply, manchildren are convinced that the social odds stacked against them are formidable. Too few can see a future for their lives, as they have already discovered the frustrating truth, they have little to live for. By all accounts, their solutions are proving fatal.

Add on to that Kunjufu's admonition that even when black males fall victim to homicide, their deaths may not strictly count as a homicide. It might just be "death by suicide." What that simply means is: "He provokes others to do what he, himself, did not do, that to kill him as a way of killing himself, as a way of committing suicide."[38] He recommends a reassessment of these homicidal deaths in order that a greater sensitivity might inform the black community as to how our manchildren are seeking their execution at another's hand. At the same time, the black community must carefully monitor claims of our young men having a death wish to defend the mounting body bags that accrue from law enforcement personnel "doing their jobs," as well as from lethal gang and drug activities. This elevated trend toward young black male morbidity, with gun violence and suicide on the rapid incline, grows ever adept at recruiting life-threatening collaborators.[39] Drug and alcohol use, though little explored in statistical terms in this project, is inextricably linked with incarceration among youth. The extent to which drug and alcohol use determines delinquent behavior has not been decided here, but research points to the fact that such use is a "major subtext" for incarcerated youth. What this signifies is that behavioral changes among youth or rehabilitation efforts on their behalf cannot progress in any effective manner without critical attention to drug treatment rather than punitive law enforcement.[40] Respected researchers M.A. Bortner and Linda M. Williams, in their trenchant text *Youth in Prison,* discovered from prison interviews:

> Drugs are ubiquitous and integral to the youths' everyday lives. Drugs are seen as a vehicle for entertainment as well as an escape from the disappointments and hardships of everyday life. For some youths, the months spent in prison are among the few that they have been "straight" in recent years. [41]

In these two nations, before manchildren is a situation where politicians and policy-makers refuse to admit that black youth's social problems are inextricably bound to society's. While much of black youth's behavior might be aptly assessed as problematic, it is also symptomatic of the social and economic retrenchment accosting the U.S. welfare state. Since the late 70's and early 80's to today, national, state, and local budget cuts to social and educational programs and services for youth widened the circle of social disadvantage for black youth, and keep them at a distinct disadvantage. This nation saw the intensification of the attack upon the poor during those

tough Reagan years. On top of that, in recent years poor communities witnessed the billions of dollars in tax breaks by the Bush administration to the wealthy, as well as the short-sighted budget cuts for services and programs intended to mitigate those designed-to-fail conditions that harass the lives of manchildren. Denying them "hope and opportunity [which] will result in too many more Black and Latino children getting sucked into a Cradle to Prison Pipeline crisis."[42]

The marginal social safety net—characteristic of the latter half of the twentieth century U.S. welfare state, and necessary to the survival and protection of the poor and vulnerable citizens like children, in effect—is being shredded for a privatized corporate, country club political climate, favored by the Bush's White House, where wealth rather than citizenship decides who gains access to the limited resources of this government.[43] (Victims of Hurricane Katrina[44] vouched for the veracity of that statement before the world stage.) Can we wonder why President Barack Obama accused the Bush administration of doing nothing to defuse a "'quiet riot'"[45] among blacks that threatens to disrupt business as usual in this nation? With the removal of the last line of defense, young black males in these feeble communities are made ever more aware of their vulnerability.[46] It is a recipe ripe for failure for far too many of them. Last of all, when their crisis conditions are tied to joblessness in disastrous numbers, they end up systematically detached from mainstream society, which further ensures their sustained marginalization and disposability.[47]

In the end, lost to drug wars, gang activities, and ruthless homicides, manchildren are barred extensively from life chances that are unrestricted to the rest of the American citizenry.[48] Perhaps, this explains why it's far easier for society to discard manchildren as lost causes, than to peer deeper into foul circumstances infecting their lives with uncensored misery and despair; easier for society to crucify them in the flesh, than bestow their unpromised lives with rightful human possibility. Frustrated and battling a chronic sense of hopelessness, these manchildren understand one reality irrefutably: "For a youth with no other hope in a system that excludes them, the gang becomes their corporation, college, religion, and life."[49]

Personal Responsibility

Given the gravity of social circumstances entrapping young black males, cautious restraint is strongly urged at the hands of policy-makers, social stakeholders, elected officials and the civic-minded in brandishing that crude language of choice as a punitive weapon against manchildren. As already established, manchildren do not participate in a unfettered choice economy. Rather, they are deeply mired in a complex web of hostile conditions, some not of their choosing, many not of their own making, despite the overdone rhetoric about personal accountability. And even though the reader might query again and again: "What about his responsibility?" Perchance, in deference to the manchild's limited choice economy, I have erred on the side of social responsibility. For no matter the highly touted rhetoric of personal accountability by the powerful societal elites, both black and white, the odds stacked against manchildren are visceral and forbidden. These limit their ability to succeed in a society based upon the unequal application of liberal notions of choice and freedom in America. As opposed to more moral demonization, I argue that black manchildren deserve a fair and critical appraisal of that so-called liberal notion of "choice," which, in actual fact, truncates their life chances and operates at an alarming level of punitive spitefulness in public policy to incarcerate their future.

At the same time, I deeply fear giving manchildren a pass for not seizing their lives with their best potential. Who will save them, if not themselves? But, in that the national conversation has been so one-sided, mean-spirited and antagonist to them and their human fulfillment, justice demands a fairer portrayal of their hard-earned lives. Herein lies my commitment to articulate a pressing argument to counter the punitive posture of powerful social stakeholders threatening, if not punishing, these young men's very human right to life.[50]

What these many essays especially seek to stress is the fact that young black males navigate a minefield of social impediments without the necessary institutional support or systematic intervention to guide and protect them. What they need most is substantial public policy intervention into their disadvantaged circumstances. Repairing the gaping breaches in their economically neglected neighborhoods and raising up their failed schools head the list of priorities. Yet public policy intervention on their behalf fights a losing battle. It competes intensely with what this government does abroad, like that unpopular war in Iraq siphoning off domestic dollars from the Katrina rebuilding project; the annual loss of American jobs, shipped aboard to places such as Mexico and Southeast Asia; the shredding of the national safety net with irresponsible tax breaks to the rich forfeits the future of already disenfranchised manchildren; and all around this general malaise to society's vulnerable. Needless to say, our manchildren are losing the battle to the priorities of this nation's global corporate agenda.

Finally, manchildren need compassionate community hands to guide them into better decision-making practices. Making mistakes and learning from them are part of life's training ground for mature adulthood. In that all important sense, they are no different from other youth. Only, in this nation, the margin of error for black youth's misdeeds grows even slimmer indeed. Because they are poor and black and male and young, making mistakes has come with an unforgiving penalty: anticipated death, anytime incarceration. At this stage in their vulnerable lives, public outcries for their immediate punishment and banishment to prison or juvenile incarceration, if they're among the lucky ones, do not rehabilitate them into model citizens, but possibly hardened criminals. They need true options and real life chances beyond so-called criminal justice solutions.

As a final note, for lives that are daily battered with unfair life odds, when death and incarceration vie for manchildren's final resting place, not only should this grieve the human spirit over this senselessness waste and what a human tragedy, but it should also mobilize concerned citizens of every race, and surely their community of native birth, to consider what we can do to stem the tide of this brewing crisis—if it's not already too late for another stolen generation.

CHAPTER 1

Manchild in the Promised Land
An American Dream or Nightmare

He's looking at me. His eyes were open real wide.... The first thing that came to my mind was, 'Finish him.' He was choking and gagging on blood in his throat and blood coming out of his nose.... 'Now look at you, you b—-ass nigger!' Extending the pistol, I pumped 10 more shots into Davis's head and body, then ran, laughing, back to where Tyrone had parked, next to Peace Baptist Church.

Russell Wallace, 16 years old

Each time I shot someone, each time I put another gun on the set, each time I successfully recruited a combat soldiers, I was congratulated by my older homeboys. When I went home I was cursed for not emptying the trash. Trash? Didn't Mom know who I was? Apparently not.

Monster Kody Scott, Monster

A voice of conscience about his own lost generation, Claude Brown's coming-of-age autobiographical novel,[51] *Manchild in the Promised Land*, witnesses to the daily wager of manchildren to beat the urban odds in America's unpromised land. Single-mindedly, his novel tracks his rapid collision course with early death. It tells of Brown's own perilous sojourn through Harlem's ghetto streets, swarming with their fair share of drugs and guns, with violence plotted as a way of life, of the ubiquitous street crime economy—lamented as the death of black America—and ready to entrap any unsuspecting manchild-recruit. In mean, crime-ridden streets was where Brown's lot had already been cast when little more than a boy-child. Aptly said, from the fractured shards of his own life-and-death struggle, *Manchild* schools out-of-touched America about the ugly realism of black teen demise and anticipated death in a mid-twentieth century Harlem. But gaining that gut-wrenching insight into how the manchild battled for life in newly declared urban war zones was not a painless read. A 1960's public had to suffer the stinging wrath of Brown's blunt honesty; a cost negligible, when considering the soul crimes committed against his own generation. Set in broad strokes, Brown's gripping accounts of being marooned in an urban tragedy drive the pulsating beat of this essay. With little detour, his life narrative commentaries the historic continuity of the life trials of manchildren and their hellish struggle for life in blood-scarred trenches in today's urban America.

*

Throughout the 429 pages of his masterful work, Brown's uncompromising street candor rips apart any Ellis Island liberty façade, censors its rhetoric, and exposes America's combat zones, a.k.a. the black unpromised land. What Brown prophesies, with little pretense at euphemism, is that for the sons and daughters of former sharecroppers, the American dream was never theirs to cherish. The epic reach of that Harlem street prophet yet witnesses to the scale of these crisis conditions menacing young black males just as heartless today. What his narrative eyewitnesses to most brutally is that when it comes to the manchild in the U.S., with all this nation's benevolent promises to white immigrants' progress, in its onerous midst throughout urban homelands lie graveyards overflowing with black death and demise. Was this the promised land that Malcolm X judged to be the "American nightmare?" The narrator of Brown's book, "Sonny Boy," answers with a defiant yes; he sets out, page by page, in his riveting manchild's tale to defend the truth of his own intimate perceptions through the unforgettable telling of his risky life trials. Woven as they are with righteous outrage, frustrating incidents of parasitic black-on-black violence, the portrayals of fragile families on the brink of collapse from the coldhearted stresses of urban transition, his own notoriety in Harlem's seedy underside society, and always those rare moments of uncommon grace, comes a hard-knocked life narrative not meant to be romanticized.

Whether Brown's straight-talk narrative tells us the whole truth, we'll never know. What he does tease out about his alarming boyhood and teenage experiences assures us that the siege of black death has not been rescinded. Conditions designed-for-black youth failure—that ubiquitous drug economy, uncaring school systems, impoverished homes, broken families, and the ever-present surplus of black misery and pain—savage black youth just as merciless today. Only increasing in intensity is that endless flow of handguns, supplying the fire power of black death.[52] Of what Brown does tell readers and what we do know of the hostile conditions cursing black inner-city young life into a kind of social profanity are enough to make the black community stand up and take action to secure the future of the next manchild.

As for Brown's generation, death by drug overdose casualties tolled as high as death by gunshot or knife combat. For today's manchild, because of the ample supply of unregulated handguns set loose on our city streets, gun violence counts considerably more for the unprecedented youth slaughter in the black community. A voice from out of the rubble of the 1992 L.A. riots witnesses to the heart-numbing despair, misdirected as vicious rage among gun-wielding black children: "I have lived in South Central Los Angeles all my life. I grew up on Florence and Normandie. That is part of my territory. I was recruited into the Crips at the ripe old age of eleven.... I have shot numerous people and have been shot seven times myself."[53] That very kind of compelling first-hand knowledge pieces together the rawest details of Brown's rebel tale. But even more to the point, his narrative earnestly profiles the fault lines of two different American worlds, paraded as a contradiction in the manchild's short-lived life, and alerts us to the hostile divide that defeats any misled hope of a real promised land.

Perhaps though, his greatest legacy may be how his urban trials function as a truth-telling deterrent from spawning "more dangerous Claude Browns."[54]

Though published during a decade of civil rights unrest, to a nation's shame, the urban trials that Brown survived does not retreat into a timely irrelevance with respect to the plight of young black males. His bold work refuses the burial of obsolescence. Frighteningly uncanny is how it parallels the present-day plight of manchildren. To the point, that forty odd years later, the bleak social commentary rendered by Brown about his generation—"It seemed as though most of the cats that we'd come up with just hadn't made it. Almost everybody was dead or in jail"[55]—is a self-fulfilled prophecy by manchildren of the nineties and today: "This is tough on me…because so many of my former high school friends have died or are in jail." [56] "As a survivor among the dying and the dead, Brown tells it like it was and like it still is," credits the compliment of one perceptive commentator. His scantly-clad autobiography affirms the continuity of the life's wager—of manchildren in each generation—to survive America's combat zones, because they are black, because they are male, and because they are young and poor. Hounded by random, premature death, the inescapable clutches of certain incarceration, and that ever simmering black rage kept on an even shorter leash raise the risk factors of every manchild born in the ghetto.

In the end, with special appreciation, one has to admire Brown's belligerent "will to survive,"[57] which eventually overthrows his victimization in many of its arduous social permutations. Somewhere in the beginning of the novel, he metaphorically casts his own life situation as "blood and vomit" and, in fact, that very morbidity haunts him throughout its rapidly moving pages. Trying to outrun the shadow of his own impending death sentence might explain, in part, Brown's fierce sense of urgency impressed all through his urban confessions. And in the heroic end, he does, that is—escape. Against frightful odds, Brown claims an urban success story. He earns a college degree at one of the most prestigious, historically black colleges, Howard University, and later a law degree. Not to glorify the messenger ahead of his message, it's how Brown chronicles the descent of his lost generation—their being alienated in their dying and despair through perilous city streets—that captures the wholehearted imagination of this chapter.

*

As it does to every black manchild, Brown's loss of innocence comes far too early. Given the harsh brutality made ordinary to many an existence and the certainty of an unpromised tomorrow, such frontline conditions age manchildren beyond their few years. Reflecting back upon his young life, one manchild reminisces,

> Certainly I had little respect for life when practically all my life I had seen people assaulted, maimed, and blown away at very young ages, and no one seemed to care. I recognized early that where I lived, we grew and died in dog years. Actually some dogs outlived us.[58]

Neighborhood prophets, according to Brown, had already forecast his imminent doom long before his 21 birthday. Having mastered minor and major apprenticeship skills in Harlem's illicit trades—gang leader, thief, a chronic liar, dope pusher, hustler and his excessive curiosity about any vice that came naturally to street life survival—can we wonder why? From page one, with his street-hardened ways, Brown was bent upon proving the community elders right. All of thirteen, and his urban tale erupts with a bullet stuck fast in his belly, penance for a youthful indiscretion—burglary: "There was a bullet in me trying to take my life…," Brown accuses, stretched out in a leaky pool of his own bleeding mortality. By age nine Brown possesses a reputation for being a little, tough guy. As he recalls, "By the time I was nine years old, I had been hit by a bus, thrown into the Harlem River (intentionally), hit by a car, severely beaten with a chain. And I had set the house afire."[59] At the ripe old age of fourteen, Brown had already reconciled himself to one unforgiving reality: "…That all cats like me ever did was smoke reefers and steal and fight and maybe eventually get killed…. I wasn't going any place but to jail or someplace like that."[60] Looming ever large, as his words bitterly betray, loiters a self-fulfilling prophecy for manchildren then and now. But casting themselves as larger-than-life fiends was a malevolent image pilfered from society's bankrupted stereotypes, recklessly profiling black youth. Already in his young teen years, Brown had intuited that black male children are born beneficiaries of spirit-murder, policed by the social contract that their earthly passage will be brief, angry, and a furious struggle through hell, where only the lucky alley "cats" make it to manhood.

His novel accuses no death angel of ravaging the black community of its power, its hope, its tomorrows. Nor does Brown erect any victim-blaming memorials. Certainly, he has every right to; for his urban odyssey chillingly interrogates the limits of personal agency to overthrow social plagues conspiring with his premature death. But his rank criticism does not stop there. His intent is not to excuse the moral dereliction of a nation. Squarely at the center of his bitter protest was the inadequacy of social systems to respond fairly and justly to black youth's survival, fathered by rabid racism and unequal access to America's golden fields of opportunity. On one such occasion, during a sentencing hearing, Brown and his adolescent crew were told by the presiding judge, "I'm going to give you boys another chance." Their appearance in court, this time, was owed to being apprehended by the local authorities while Brown and his friends were caught red-handed breaking into the local A & P. At the hearing, Brown startled the judge and himself with his reprimand: "…I don't know why or what happened, but I heard myself say, 'Man, you not givin' us another chance. You givin' us the same chance we had before.'" From his youth Brown had discerned that their untimely demise was helped along by a callous state indifference to the unequal life chances of young black males. This surely would explain his scornful dismissal of the white judge's so-called show of grace as being only hypocritical rhetoric. Returning them to their crime-infested environment was not an improved life chance, nor expanded choices, but only an opportunity to dig a deeper hole for their early burial. Throughout the novel, incidents such as this bore "terrifying witness" to just how cursed their young lives really were, ill-fated with little choice at all.[61]

As a manchild raised in America's mean city streets, the life chances of Brown were just as slim, precarious, and uncertain as the next black boy whom he grew up with in the drug-infested, rough streets of Harlem at 146th Street and Eight Avenue, as are those of young black males all over urban America today. "He was gunned down for being in the wrong place at the wrong time.... I just stood there, looking at my friend's blood on the floor. He had never harmed anyone in his entire life," a manchild diaries from Long Beach, California.[62] What choice did Brown have? What of black youth like once gang member, Monster Kody Scott? who weighs in on behalf of his own defense:

> To be in a gang in South Central when I joined—
> and it is still the case today—is the equivalent
> of growing up in Grosse Pointer, Michigan, and
> going to college: everyone does it. Those who
> don't aren't part of the fraternity. And as with
> everything from a union to a tennis club, it's
> better to be in than out.[63]

Relentlessly tied to powerful social realities, the manchild's world of choices is bound to the limited choices, if not choiceless choices, already set in motion to contain his life within the narrow borders of a Harlem or South Central L.A. "hood". Black youth understand that unequivocally, even when they can't articulately counter all the punitive political rhetoric dooming their lives to a criminal cage and rage. As one manchild after another bears witness to the harrowing plight of being a young black male: "To be a Black boy turned out by the horrific conditions of America's gutters is to be a Black boy fighting for survival every minute of your life."[64]

With despair common as a routine fact of young black male life, manchildren's disaffection from American society shows up in their delinquent behavior, stifled as they are with a runaway pessimism about improving their life chances. And though they display a childish bravado in the face of dismal life prospects, manchildren of today are afraid—afraid of the possibility of going to adult prison, of payback gang violence, and most assuredly, of dying a cold-hearted death. How a nation converts their despair into an imagination of hope is the challenge.

*

Up close and personal, actually too close for comfort much of the times, Brown's scorching-hot urban guide takes us to his side of town; once there, Brown orients the reader's gaze to the wanton conditions strangling young black men in America's gutters and inner-cities' killing fields. He takes no prisoners. With bold strokes and in his "hip" sixties' lingo, Brown renders inescapable the parasitic survival made instinctive to street culture, of drugs and jail upon black male autonomy, and his own sisyphus search for young black manhood. Hear some of his own internal moral dilemma:

> I felt bad. Nobody had ever stuck me up or s— like that. I knew that this would get around, and you couldn't deal any drugs if you were going to be letting cats stick you up and take it. I knew that I'd have to get a gun, and that when cats heard about it…they would also want to hear that the guy had been killed. This was the way the people in our set did things…. I didn't want to, but I knew I had to get another piece and find that cat.[65]

An early reviewer of his book described it as a "guided tour to hell conducted by a man who broke out." Brown's uncensored point of view confronts the reader with where and how the other half lives, surviving by mean margins indeed. "If somebody hadn't died from an O.D., somebody had gotten killed trying to get some drugs or something crazy like that." To his credit, his work does not skip over the sordid details of his boyhood spent in Harlem streets among gang members, prostitutes, hustlers and addicts—even killers. Brown is purposeful not to cast himself as a goody-too-shoe choir boy either. But the black teen male society loves to fear, to demonize, stereotype and reject unapologetically.

What reigns pitifully clear, though, is that the lowest common denominator familiar to poor, black urban life still rages with little decline since Brown's 1965 classic work. Having only increased in fury in twenty-first century urban America is evidenced by the killing fields of today's L.A., Philadelphia, Chicago, Washington, D.C., or Baltimore.[66] Caught up in all the paces of street machismo, the added blood income of drug trafficking, dodging the community's crossfire of gun violence, and the sure confidence of being incarcerated, raiders of death still hound manchildren with voracious fury. Little has changed to secure our children's future. Whether a reader is prepared to admit the terrible truth of the gritty sights beheld or not is immaterial. Willingly or not, Brown's insider knowledge obliges his readers to concede a devastating fact stable throughout the everyday and every night, life–and-death struggles of the manchild—that is, there are few demilitarized zones in urban life. Even those with the strongest iron-clad will to resist the destructive elements of ghetto life can die at the willful hand of its hard-core culture. An updated blood narrative of how the manchild dies, ever at-risk, no matter the premature efforts to forestall an untimely demise on his and his family's part.

Blair Holt was the 16-year-old son of a Chicago firefighter and a police officer. An honor student at Julian High School, Blair was killed the afternoon of May 10 while using his body to shield a classmate when a gang member opened fire on a crowded CTA bus. While riding home, a teen boarded the bus, aimed at a rival gang member at the back of the vehicle, and opened fire, according to police record. Caught in the line of fire, Blair was fatally wounded. Four other students were struck but survived…. As Rev. Jesse Jackson told mourners, "Blair attracts us because he wasn't a gangbanger. His blood wasn't full of drugs. The gun wasn't in his hands."[67]

For many of his unlucky cohorts, for whom Brown grieves:

> ...I just couldn't go to the funeral. Butch was a good friend of mine, but it was too much. I was getting tired of funerals. I was getting tired of seeing cats I knew die from overdoses, cats who had promising futures, who had good heads on their shoulders....

A manchild of the twenty-first century likewise mourns the memory of a friend murdered in a recent drive-by: "My friend shouldn't have died that night. He should still be here having fun and enjoying life with the rest of us. He's not the first nor will he be the last friend that I lose. I've lost many friends, friends who have died in an undeclared war."[69] Among manchildren, where does this pointless dying end? Absent public accessed to the vaults of the American dream, their private promised land hoards a minefield of social vices with its aimless rage, that hemorrhaging hopelessness relieved only by an escapist addiction, and a casual violence preying tirelessly upon black male vulnerability.

Although baptized into a culture of self-perpetuating violence from his youth, Brown never upgrades to one of the "bad niggers" in the community: "I was growing up now, and ...I would soon be expected to kill a nigger if he mistreated me, like Rock, Bubba, Williams, and Dewdrop had.... I knew now that I had to keep up with these cats; if I didn't I would lose my respect in the neighborhood...." Urged upon him was the street demand to either "evolve or perish." "I knew that I was going to have to get a gun sooner or later and that I was going to have to make my new rep and take my place along with the bad niggers of the community." The violent choice that Claude Brown escaped befalls black youth today at even deadlier numbers, because street life assures little middle ground to debate the indisputable law of the concrete jungle. One of the fortunate ones, before it was too late, Brown detoured from that inevitable path. At seventeen, he was "ready to retire from it. I'd already had ten or eleven years at it." For breaking his freefall into hardcore criminality, he credits Wiltwyck Reformed School and most notably, the earnest support of his mentor, Dr. Ernest Papanek, the psychologist and director—whom Brown pays humble tribute in his novel as "probably the smartest and the deepest cat I had ever met"—for his social redemption. To aid his personal transformation, Brown chose to move away from his Harlem "hood" to overcome the temptations of backsliding into crime. He describes it fittingly as "away from fear, toward challenges, towards the positive anger that I think every young man should have." A kind hand of intervention aided Brown in discovering the moral courage and strength to pull away from a life of crime to make that choice to save his life.

Later generations of more dangerous Claude Browns, who are all the more in desperate need of society's humane intervention, flinch not from the horror of the executioner's duty expected of them. For these manchildren, killing is a part of paying dues; it's part and parcel of the conditions and circumstances that breed these youth's identities. In gang life it is especially evident: "Every time I jump somebody in and make someone a part of our gang, it's another baptism: They give us their life and we give them a new one. All they have to do is prove they're down.... Risking life, dodging or taking bullets, and pulling triggers."[70] Recycling the everyday drama of survival by sheer wit and fortitude, the harsh code of street survival stays ever at the fore of a gang banger's mind. In actual fact, for many of them, the law of their concrete jungle urges murder as a necessary prerequisite to their living. Disconnected from society as they are and burdened with this rabid social alienation, better understood is their motto of life: "Killin' and not caring, and dyin' without fear. It's love for your set and hate for the enemy. You hear what I'm sayin'?"[71] Although society scourges them as gang members, their environment preys upon them as any boy soldier roaming in a "Third World" undeclared conflict zone.

Surviving one man-made hell after another, manchildren grow tough scabs upon their emotions to lessen their self-reproach, and to numb the fears associated with honing their survival instincts. At eleven or twelve, our children suffer from combat fatigue. Some retire for an early break in suicide. One close buddy admits: "I think he was just tired of his life—the way it was going. Things weren't right."[72] Whether a gang banger or not, young black males know that they are on the frontlines in defense of their lives, their human right to survival. Too often that means they survive by "any means necessary." Already, they have understood a fated fact of their living: that killing and dying are part of the social contract enforced on them by their external conditions.

> I figured I had to find a way to protect myself from these fools, and the only way was to get a gun. At school, some of my friends have been talking about a homie being strapped. I asked them where he got it from, and they told me that some guy sold it to him. With memories of my homies getting smoked and all my problems on the way home, I decided to get one. It's so damn easy to get a gun; it's like getting bubble gum from the corner liquor store. All you need is $25.[73]

With the proliferation of unregulated handguns, more-than-ever youth are finding it easier to settle casual and not so casual arguments with reckless death. As one manchild laments, "They don't fight one-on-one or nothin'...."

Finally, forsaking that instinctual call of the streets, though Brown fondly embraces those mean streets as home: "I remember when I ran away from shelters, places that they sent me to, here in the city. I never ran away with the thought in mind of coming home. I always ran away to get back to the streets.... To me, home was the streets."[74] The sum total of his life was so roughly tied to the streets or hood, bonded as he was by his own shed blood, by a harsh code of acceptance, street respect, an unbrokered sense of lawless power in his and his friends' hands. I am one reader who empathizes with that overwhelming sense of geographical enclosure imitating the life limitations imposed upon Brown's potential, that of his generation, and that of manchildren today. After all is told, he was not the last manchild being "squashed to death" by urban blight and the coterie of related problems in neighborhoods suffering dereliction. Such injurious conditions can be traced directly to the lack of political will on the part of various state and federal lawmakers to revitalize these ailing urban communities. Where are manchildren to go then, hemmed in as they are by the crisscrosses of a main street and cross street, interned in their claustrophobic ghetto jungle reality? Others are not as generous as Brown in their memory of the streets. They recall the depth of the abyss to which their lives felt condemned. "I'm 18 in a country with no path / 4 a young unaddicted Black youth with a Dream," as a frustrated young black rapper rhymes.

*

When going to jail was an everyday fact of life, even then, Brown had divined what society deemed as the lawful place for the black manchild—death or the "Tombs"— penitentiary. He chronicles with uncanny certainty black youth being apprehended at some point and remanded to juvenile reform facilities. Even then, the cradle-to-prison pipeline had begun its pernicious encroachment upon young black male life, now in full swing. Given this present punitive climate aligned against black youth, transfer to adult courts for prosecution grows every likely. Far too many manchildren, one out of every three African Americans born today faces the prospect of jail at some point in his life. One of the lucky ones was given probation. Like this teenage writer from the *Freedom Writers Diary*, he lets slip his tough-guy mask to acquaint the world with his youthful vulnerability:

> When I arrived at juvenile hall it was scary. They treated me like a criminal.... I was unlike any of the people surrounding me. Caged like beasts were murderers, rapists, gangsters, and robbers. The first night was the scariest. I heard sounds I had never heard before. Inmates banging on walls, throwing up their gang signs, yelling out who they were and where they are from. I cried on my first night.[75]

For many more manchildren, less consideration is given to the severity of the crime or to the criminal history of the offender. Once in the hands of the criminal justice system, our young are tried and sentenced as a matter of due process, even first time non-violent offenders. This trend grows ever common to the criminal justice process for black youth.[76] An excellent reader, *Youth In Prison*, carefully evaluates how "public figures gain political capital by portraying delinquent youths as a primary cause of societal problems and by advocating 'get tough' policies as the answer to those problems."[77] The critique by Bortner and Williams exposes how literally all incarcerated youth are collapsed into this generalized mug shot of a violent, recalcitrant, and inhumane monster. When, in fact, statistics prove the stereotype false, most incarcerated youth are non-violent offenders. In their final words, Bortner and Williams adopt the position that such portrayals serve ideological and political ends, not the treatment needs of hurting children.

The fact is, there is political currency in sensationalizing the young black male image as a "bogey man" or "super-predator" that covets handcuffing for the sake of resolving so-called "out of control" social problems. His becomes an image that is easy to manipulate for increased support for law-and-order departments and indeed to fuel the prison industrial complex. Any number of causes can be readily rhetoricized for lawmakers and politicians for the sake of expediency in the criminalization of young black males. Rather than believe a media prone to sensationalism, the black community needs to see through the smoking mirror of political rhetoric to baldly assess its ramifications for our community's future. Manchildren are casualties in an undeclared drug war throughout forsaken urban communities. Their vulnerability is aggravated by difficult domestic circumstances and callous external institutions like the failed school systems and the untrustworthy criminal justice system, with unemployment in the black community at an all-time high for black youth. Uncaring social realities are committed to exacerbating their tenuous survival.

In the case of scarce employment, there is an appalling lack of mainstream mentoring experiences for our young teens to transition into more profitable job occupations in New York City. To gain a sense of that loss, frequently the only job a 16-year old can get after school is hawking candy on the subway. This is Wayne's self-introduction:

> Excuse me ladies and gentlemen. Sorry for the interruption. But may I have your attention, please. My name is Wayne. And I'm not selling candy for a basketball team. But for myself, to have a little money in my pocket. I would gladly appreciate it if you were to buy some. It's only one dollar. The candy I have left is MM peanuts. Thank you for your time. God bless you. Have a safe trip.
>
> Wayne 16 years old

I admire his bootstrap initiative. Unfortunately, for the vast majority of black teens, they no longer bag groceries in grocery stores, nor clean small mom-and-pop family restaurants, nor make deliveries for small retail businesses in the neighborhood; they are the economically forgotten.[78] Not receiving that essential "training for life experiences" dooms many of them to a headlong plunge into the abyss of black crime and criminality. Joblessness figures precipitously in deciding the fate of a vulnerable generation of black children.

In Brown's urban confessions is cast a well-founded suspicion upon the effectiveness of this nation's penal system to adequately rehabilitate juvenile offenders. A friend from the old days, Brown's "boy" Reno, confesses to a disturbing truth, "Every time I went there, I learned a little more. When I go to jail now, Sonny, I live, man. I 'm right at home. That's the good part about it. If you look at it, Sonny, a cat like me is just cut out to be in jail."[79] When the manchild re-emerges, still-born and atrophied of social and job skills, to try to survive productively in mainstream society, he is, in effect, coerced into a false nostalgia for his familiar crowded cage. This is the height of an institutional mentality, where black men are more comfortable behind metal bars than on the outside in the unruly world of everyday life.

Reno's confession pierces to the heart of the matter that's overwhelming black America: lack of juvenile rehabilitation and mounting recidivism. Once a chronic juvenile offender himself, Brown volunteers, "We all came out of Warwick better criminals." He should know. His first-hand experience with the juvenile detention system did little to rehabilitate his inclination for "lying and stealing." More importantly, in decades since Brown, the structural weaknesses of the criminal justice system stressed by Brown in his narrative have only escalated into a kind of plantation politics in the nineties, and now in the twenty-first century. For instance, eleven years old Marcus F. was sentenced to the Department of Juvenile Justice for murder in 1998. About six months before his 21 birthday, he was released to a halfway house, which he later fled. Days later, he was apprehended and arrested for carjacking with an accomplice; both had loaded guns. The judge sentenced him to life in prison, along with a host of other charges for good measure. Right out of prison, and already he had a gun to carjack somebody. What was this once 11-year old child rehabilitated into, a harden criminal? A family member of that growing rank of the incarcerated, a manchild himself rails against the social injury done to children made to grow up in the juvenile prison system. His words corroborate Brown and others, and so does his angry passion toward this casual disposal of loved ones:

My cousin was convicted of murder at the age of 11. Ten years later, he fled from a program that released him outside of prison wall, but he carjacked someone when he was only a month away from finishing his sentence. Now he has just been sentenced to life in prison. I honestly don't think the prison system invests the time in the inmates to make them better people. If anything, it's an incubator of violence and hate.

From one strong opinion, once inside the juvenile justice system he verifies that there is little pretense about attempts to rehabilitate black youth. "The juvenile tank has got to be the most blatant exercise the state has ever devised for corrupting, institutionalizing, and creating recidivism in youths."[80] When transferred to adult court, the outcomes projected are even more grim.

Although youths transferred to the adult criminal justice system are more likely to be convicted and incarcerated, they are more likely to re-offend, [to] re-offend earlier, and to commit more serious subsequent offenses than those who remain in the juvenile system.[81]

Who will save once manchildren like Marcus F., from themselves, from one another, and from a callous world that has little tolerance for their misdeeds? Although the victim was unharmed, she was emphatic: "This is someone the community needs to be free of."[82] What will we do about the thousands upon thousands of young black males like him, who have been institutionalized almost longer than free, returned to our community just briefly to be recaptured as recidivists?

In truth, maybe the intimate perspective of Reno finding jail to be "almost like a family" or "home" casts a crude spotlight on certain psychological and emotional influences at play that would foil the manchild's re-entry into society, and may contribute excessively to the high recidivism rate in the black community. From the other side, his recidivism is also symptomatic of the inadequate programmatic responses to deflect social triggers that "lie in wait" to ensnare him once on the "outside." For upon his release from prison, consider what the manchild return to. Job readiness and training programs? GED classes? No, the manchild returns home to the same old battlegrounds: relentless poverty, intensified violence, a home rife with domestic disturbances, the same old "hood" enemies; and on top of that, he winds up selling and abusing drugs for quick cash, because who wants to hire a juvenile offender? Without criminal records, job opportunities are scare for black youth in this downsized economy. What can we reasonably expect for those who do? Disastrously, the manchild rejoins the very same "trigger" infested context that led to his initial round-up, prosecution and incarceration, which almost assures his recidivism.[83] Perhaps, this is redundant, but where are the tangible investments for young black men coming out of prison? What more can we do, must we do, as a community to ensure that those who choose to go straight can seize the opportunity?

Finally, criminalization accomplishes the contentious social and political goal of banishing manchildren to an incarcerated world that begrudges them a second chance and refuses any moral measure of redemption or rehabilitation for their battle-torn lives. Its quick-fixed criminal "solution" has also hastened the social death[84] of this very same population. What I mean here is that incarceration sets in motion harsh conditions of estrangement and disenfranchisement related to their release, borne by manchildren who receive felony convictions—from severely limited employment opportunities to being disenfranchised of voting rights. As adult males, many end up homeless and totally alienated from the mainstream of society, doomed to an infallible recidivism.

*

Increasingly today, although they received less attention in Brown's true-to-life narrative, prisons are serving the oppressive interests of the corporate and political elites.[85] Right now, they have evolved as the right arm of economic development in the U.S., and are, in fact, the housing development plan for blacks and the poor in the twenty-first century. Why? "...White communities, where many of the prisons are located, witnessed a significant boom in business, including new employment opportunities."[86] As late as the twenty-first century, in a nation that bills itself as the "homeland" and "headquarters" of world freedom, its greatest defender, although America comprises 5 percent of the world's population, its jails and prisons house more than 25 percent of the world's prisoners. [87] The arresting aspect of this is that the black community has the "worst imprisonment odds in the world, one out of eight prisoners on the planet is African American, although African Americans make up only about one-half of one percent of humanity. 'Such heights of racist barbarity are not reached by accident.'"[88] No, not the proud beneficiaries of the American dream, but blacks are the targeted preys of the American Gulag.[89] This dire situation facing the black community today strongly echoes Dr. King's scathing moral critique charged at America over a half-century ago. In essence, it shows how little this nation has matured on the moral front: In King's sentiments, the well-being of a nation is not measured by its scientific-technological advances, but by its most vulnerable citizen. America cannot continue to represent itself as a human right saint while massacring the potential of its black children, the poor and vulnerable, incarcerating them out of sight to impersonate on the world stage how benevolent it is, while callously under-developing the soul wealth of its own nation with reckless neglect, demonstrating a flagrant disregard for the empowerment needs of the truly disinherited.

In states such as Alabama, Mississippi, Texas and Florida, ex-felons have permanently lost their right to vote.[90] Due to felony convictions, 1.46 million black men out of a total voting population of 10.4 million have become disenfranchised.[91] "Is this how the "Ole South shall rise again?" A new historical moment with the same supremacist agenda, in this case: dilute the collective power of the black vote through discrimination against felon offenders, in specifically, against those who have paid their debt to society.

Even then, Brown was adamant about not being tagged with a rap sheet.

> One thing began to scare me more than anything else about jail. This was the fact that if I went to jail and got that sheet on me, any time I decided that I didn't want to go the crime way, that I wanted to do something that was straight, I'd have a lot of trouble doing it behind being in jail. I didn't want that sheet on me, and I knew if I kept hanging around Harlem I was going to get busted for something jive, something like smoking reefers. And it would be a shame for somebody to get busted for smoking reefers and get a sheet and have his whole life f—d [change mine] up.[92]

In the twenty-first century, "debt paid to society" echoes as meaningless rhetoric for black ex-offenders or parolees. Their rehabilitated status carries little redemption when past convictions as felons damn them as society's perpetual outsiders, begrudged a second chance. Not so for their white brothers:

> I have observed that many whites here seem unfazed by their plight in prison. They regard confinement merely as a temporary restraint from

their usual lives. And they face the future with optimism, confident that they have only to slip on a coat and tie, get a haircut, and shave for the establishment to forgive their transgressions.... But most blacks look ahead with apprehension, afraid that we may never be forgiven for our crimes—or the color of our skin.[93]

Case in point, reasons for the verdict of acquittal that came down from the 2007 lynching of Sean Bell and the attempt by the NYPD to "mob" murder his friends, according to Judge Arthur Cooperman, were "'inconsistent testimony, courtroom demeanor and *rap sheets* of the prosecution witnesses...had the effect of eviscerating' their credibility" (italics added). Coldblooded killers, these men were not; could the same be said for the officers who fired off fifty shots? A second chance and having paid one's debt to society boast outright hypocrisy meant absolutely nothing in the broad scheme of the trial. Bell's friends were being tried again without formal indictments, in actuality, tried again for the same offenses. Though they were victims, they would forever be marked perpetrators.[94] A thin kind of double jeopardy at work, in other words, because of a past "rap sheet," proposes to keep black men in bondage to a hostile and unforgiving penal system. How can they, how do they, ever win in a system of unequal justice?

*

If the death and incarceration statistics are any moral compass, Brown's narrative about the plight of young black males is ever relevant. Its freshness of perspective is undimmed by time transition. To that extent, it provokes far too many alarming reactions about the imperiled future of the manchild today. For this uncertain generation, still abound the hostile conditions cursing black inner-city life into a kind of social profanity. Yet in the soulful end, Brown's veteran memoir battles tirelessly with this hell-like destruction vented upon the bodies and beings of young black males as systemic as it is splintered fragments of their own personal agency.

CHAPTER 2

"Bye bye, I was never meant to live"
Saving Our Sons

"When a nigger woman brings a male child in the world, she looks at him, shakes her head, and says, 'Oh, my son, forgive me for what I've done.'"

Pimp in *Manchild in the Promised Land*

"I felt such anger—anger toward God. 'How could You let this happen to people who live like You want us to?'"

Clementina Chéry, mother of slain teen Louis Brown

"Now, she said, she's started to see what God may have had in mind when Kyron was killed. 'It was to bring this community together,' she said. To wake it up to see there is a lot of bad activities going on with shooting and drugs in this small town. People have told me, people I don't even know, that the story made them closer to their children."

Rhonda Butler, mother of 8-year old slain Kyron

A Cursed Birth

Even as he nestles softly in his mother's womb, still he is not saved. Anxiously, his black birth anticipates the manchild's death from all the unsparing coercions of early death.

As his life force labors through the fragile sanctity of her hallowed womb, what fears invade his black mother's being and grip her afflicted mind? knowing the at-risk status of premature death a black manchild is born to—dying young because adulthood status is a premium calculated far beyond his limited black reach. A black mother knows that once her son is released from the warm safety of her placenta, there are no assurances of protection from that public blight of careless violence nor the threat of constant death hounding his Achille's heel— his natural born blackness.

But the burden of sheltering their son's future is no new trial for black mothers. They have always been vigilant about protecting their sons in mean-spirited America. Indeed, the weight has been as historic as it is contemporary, and the fears as old as being black and male in this nation. Seeking out rescue advice on how to save her teen son from the vengeful wrath of street death, author and once single mother Marita Golden, in *Saving our Sons*, shares this intimate conversation she had with Joyce Ladner, a prominent black sociologist. Even upon the dawning of a new century, Ladner rehearses the unflagging fear of black mothers to Golden. "Every generation of black women has experienced tremendous anxiety about keeping their men alive." This indiscriminate condition of fear cuts across class lines to intuitively acclimate black motherhood to the irrevocable risk. *Every black mother struggles with the harassing fear of her teen son's early demise. She waits anxiously, hoping for his every return, wondering how the streets will discipline him into his frail black vulnerability.*

Such anguishing worries that prey endlessly upon his black mother's mind are grievously personal and chillingly uncertain, as they are for every black woman who is often mother and father, parenting manchildren throughout this unpromised land.

"God took the best to save the rest"

If the concerns posed about his so-called "cursed" birth appear frightening, then the justification given to atone for the manchild's early death is equally so. When a manchild is slain, often a black mother wanders around in the reaches of her religious self to find solace to heal the void caused by her son's premature demise. Patricia Gaines is one of those mothers. Her teenage son, Hank Lloyd, Jr., was gunned down by a walk-by, when mistaken as a hostile contender for drug turf while his "boys" watched on in fear for their own undervalued lives. After his funeral, his mother quietly inquires, "I looked at them and asked myself, 'What did Hank Lloyd's friends do when he was gunned down?' I realized that they had stood at an altar and vowed to establish a new relationship with God. It was a good answer."[95] Rhonda Butler, the mother of a slain 8-year old, is "determined to see that her son's death serves some [higher] purpose."[96] Not few enough black mothers testify that "he was sacrificed so that other boys could live. God took him as an offering." Lonise Bias, mother of teen and young adult sons who both died untimely deaths, chant this solace: "God took the best to save the rest."[97] What eulogy could be more befitting to annul society's faith in their son's fall from grace? Who could blame them? Only grieving black mothers can exhale a beloved lament for their fallen sons.

Of course, I can easily sympathize with why black mothers would prefer to anoint their children as emissaries of a divine mission. It counters the media's sensationalism with its folly in demonizing every black son into an incarnation of evil, cursed with an anti-social nature. But what hollow joy the black community must imbibe of that the victimization of native sons by unholy violence and senseless death can readily be sanctified by their lives being presented as an atonement to God. Every unnatural death prompted by social disregard should be mourned with gnashing of teeth and the questioning of God why, rather than resigned acceptance of the needless. Such senseless deaths! For whose sins, to whose God? what divine absurdity? God dies with every unnatural death. Crucified. If our children's splattered blood must soil asphalted city streets, let it be for the sake of a transformed present and worthwhile future, but not, for the love of God, for vain rhetoric of divine necessity. These ungodly trespasses against black sons must stop, and not be foolishly charged to the hand nor the bleeding heart of God.

Not too long ago, to my grave disappointment, I heard well-meaning but misguided civil rights leaders still spouting that same old gospel tune: "Black spirituality must redeem the soul of America."[98] Forgive me, but are our priorities mixed up? Who is redeeming our children from the sentence of street death in this same America? Why are college students being gunned down (executed) like dogs in the streets of urban America?[99] Doesn't this nation care? To make it even more personal, does the black community care? Our kids are sojourning with fear's desperation, and nobody seems to notice such a strange bedfellow for black youth.

I hate to be the skeptic, but those leaders' missionary zeal sounds like a politician's chant for re-election, a sermon to pacify the religious right, the securing of career insurance in partisan power structures, or an unhealthy case of black self-hatred, rather than expressing any adoring love for black sons. While individual vocations are being selfishly pursued on the premise of evangelizing the "soul" of this nation, right there, on the opposite side of the tracks, body bags are piling up with our future's hope. Prisons are teeming over with the silhouettes of our dark children in every cellblock. How can our community survive the loss of so many of its young, without receiving this as a death toll of our own anticipated harried demise? Let us begin, then, by saving our own sons—as that is our most righteous and redemptive calling.

"Not My Problem, Not My Son"

If the black community continues to permit this unprecedented violence perpetrated on and by our native sons be benignly explained away, what next level of atrocity upon and within the black community will our threshold of tolerance find palatable? until there is no community of which to speak. Young black men ages 14-24 make up just above one percent of the U.S. population, but they constitute about 1 percent of the murder victims and over 30 percent of the perpetrators. At this very moment, our forsaken communities are marooned in yet another dangerous Middle Passage, damp from the flow of our children's black blood. This passage is on treacherous land through littered, poop-filled city streets. If preempted actions are not taken soon, left to grieve will be only a withered remnant of a broken people. Because when we needed to be incited by moral outrage into taking strategic action, if not to our death, we rationalized our feelings into a polite denial in words like "not my problem," "not my son" or "let me mind my own business." Strangled to death by our own apathy or fears were we, while our children's life blood was poured out as a crimson ransom. When will enough be enough? and we touch our strength, our most holy rage.

Drugs and violence refuse to carry the sole blame for the desperate state of our ailing communities, hostile to young black male life. Apathy and the refusal to resist are also the genocidal agents of choice, which directly aid and abet the flow of drugs and any other ills devoted to aborting black life. Beyond just looking to God for justification for these crimes committed against our children's humanity, the accomplice status of our community and the broader society must also be interrogated on every count of "hear-no-evil, see-no-evil," and "don't get involved" complicity, when it is sorely evident that not knowing justifies too many horrific wrongs.

In an *Essence* interview with Nobel Prize Toni Morrison, also the mother of two sons, she attacks this virulent, benign neglect employed on the part of society, and even our own community, in conspiring with blighted conditions that put black children further at risk:

> The problem surfaces immediately when we hear Black children described as "them." We have been led to believe that our children are not us and that we could live well or even better if we abandoned them to their own devices or desires. We're no longer citizens, we're taxpayers, and we are being taught to vote against our own children's interests. Suddenly, poor people and their children seem to be an alien group, even to us.[100]

Morrison's point is well-taken. For to some of us, black children are strangers, unfamiliar and alien. This attitude toward them will never befriend them as mentees.

Regrettably, she identifies a central source of conflict dividing our community, which too many Black people have bought into, that is, we believe that the weakest link in the black community is our children. Buying into that mentality volunteers as a systematic seduction of our loyalty to the most basic parental instincts: the desire for our children to excel beyond the meager station of their working-class parents; to receive the rights historically denied them to enter into the wider world of opportunity; to resist the treatment of our children like wild animals, loose and untamed, prepped for capture; perhaps, mostly freed from dying an unnatural death, with a safe space to mature into their own potentiality.

The plight of young black males, in truth, is the moral barometer of the well-being of the whole black community. And we're in trouble.

Indeed, their birth burdens them with ominous social handicaps, which adversely track them into man-made enclaves of poverty, undereducation, racist violence, social alienation, and the finality of an ugly death. Under the propaganda of criminality, the black community is sold a fake bill of goods, told our children are incarcerated for the good of society, and sensationalized as the "super-predator" of society. Yet, no matter the hostile messages refusing their redemption, they deserve the human right to be saved. Even more so, society is not without guilt on its own blood-stained hands. Quite convinced, Golden faults society for its own complicit role in promoting black youth's demise: "They are not the problem but a symptom of a society in decay and decline, a society that has always used the black man, the black woman, the black child, to symbolize its worst impulse, its throbbing underside." Popular rap lyrics parlay this message from the dire straits native to where manchildren live and wage war to grow up:

Bye bye, I was never meant to live
Can't be positive, when the ghetto's where you live
Bye bye, I was never meant to be
Livin like a thief, runnin through the streets
Bye bye, and I got no place to go...
Where you find me? 16 on Death Row
Tupac Shakur

CHAPTER 3

"Abort Black Babies"
A National Call for Black Male Disposability

When my eyes were a fountain of tears the realization came
that Emmett's death was not a personal experience for me to
hug to myself and weep, but it was a worldwide awakening
that would change the course of history.

Mamie Elizabeth Till-Mobley

Arise, lift up the lad, and hold him in thine hand; for I will
make him a great nation.

(Genesis 21:18)

Not quite since the public fervor of "segregation now,
segregation tomorrow, segregation forever" stirred up a blind
racial loyalty, by the then, Governor George Wallace—[101]
making him a national iconic figure—has the nation heard a
brash repeat of brazen racism piped through national broadcast
channels into the public domain. Only recently in the public
hearing of this nation, with his own bigoted brand of racist
bravado—Secretary of Education under President Ronald
Reagan, and former drug czar appointee by President George
H.W. Bush, William Bennett let slip his savored fantasies about
young black males during his daily radio talk show, *Morning
in America.* "If you want to reduce crime, you could, if that
were your sole purpose; you could abort every black baby in
this country, and your crime rate would go down." [102]
(Immediately, what I heard in his national call to "arm" was
that greatly understated text left over from the 1990s "family
values" wars. Bennett is tired of these out-of-wedlock "black"
births ruining the so-called moral fiber of this nation. His book,
Body Count, published in the mid-1990s, said it so in 146 pages,
and now he reiterates it again for good measure in the first
decade of the twenty-first century.)[103] His ill-advised counsel

poses a grisly public policy remedy to handle some of the contention around the U.S. being the western prison-camp of the world, inmates comprised overwhelmingly of black males. When his remark sparked a spat of criticism he took jestful refuge in "just joking."[104] Talks of genocide[105] rarely are a laughing matter. Perhaps, not in the public forum to an equal degree as Bennett's, but that mean-spirited kind of like racial warfare waged by conservative moralists, politicians, criminal justice officers, social stakeholders, and the media further aggravate the crisis conditions of young black males. Racist speech of this nature, polemical for sure, attacks young black males' vulnerability in order to devalue their life chances, and sets them up in the public mind as a population deserving of disposability.

War on Terror in the Womb

Bennett's ideological parlance of "abort black babies" closely reminisced that presidential foreign policy mandate espoused after September 11 (9/11) to strike preemptively national threats. Such aggressive language of first strike, rather than statesman's diplomacy, inaugurated our nation's imperialist campaign of the war on terror.[6] Not only was President Bush's doctrine aiming at terrorist operatives like Osama bin Laden and Al-Qaeda, but the positioning of U.S. military forces for the preemptive invasion of Iraq. Although no hard data was available to connect Iraq with 9/11—or, for that matter, Saddam Hussein with Al-Qaeda activities or 9/11, the Bush's White House construed an elaborate imminent threat ploy against Hussein and his "infamous" arsenal of weapons of mass destruction, which turned up non-existent. Cleverly employed to justify America's invasion of Iraq, this fabrication of truth was imperialistically construed to convince the world community of America's right to discipline a so-called "rogue" nation; according to the administration, Iraq's threat to global security was imminent. Then, Secretary of State Colin Powell and the U.S. government defended the Bush's doomsday scenario before the 2003 United Nation Security Council. But, of course, the world community and the American people now know just how politically contrived it was.

When it comes to black youth, similar rhetoric is coming out of "respected" neoconservative quarters. Bennett, in particular, is employing an in-kind rhetorical strategy to contain another "perceived" threat: according to him, black babies must be aborted to protect America's domestic "interest." His scheme signals what hip hop author Bakari Kitwana in his book, *The Hip Hop Generation*, scourges as the harmful stigma singed in the American mind about black youth: "...African American youth, for much of the past two decades, have been deemed the problem—whether criminalized in sensational news crime reports or demonized as the architects of America's declining moral values."

Exactly now, against black fetuses, how would Bennett's dangerous preemptive strike plot work itself out in a right-wing political imagination? Is it aimed at all black fetuses or really just males? since more are in the penal system. Would white mothers of black fetuses have to comply with this public policy or State demand of abortion? In other words, does the one drop of black blood reassert its legal rule to condemn all guilty male fetuses to death? Aligned to that, what about the racial state or "condition" of the mothers? Will it be legally re-enforced, as once in slavery, to secure bloodlines through women's wombs, now to criminalize their fetus for execution? What happens if a black mother resists an immoral policy or law that demands she submits to the murder of her own black flesh? Does she become a fugitive outlaw for noncompliance and subject to being hunted down like a common thief for prosecution in withholding the cherished bounty of her womb? Without the control of her body, does she return to chattel property? At first glance, queries such as these seemingly belong more to the realm of science fiction than any real-life performance in a modern democratic state. But on second thought, what racist polemics do best is to strike an anxious fear in the heart of a vulnerable population, ever targeted for disposability. In times like these, a racial population like African Americans with their long history of living on the edge of civil liberties in America, and having endured some of this nation's worst impulses, has every right to be suspicious of polemics of this nature. Unlike so many other racial communities, as a people African Americans have always been burdened with the nagging doubt, could something as dastardly as this happen again in a liberal democracy? albeit in a different form from lynching. After all the civil rights gains, could it happen now? What seems absurd today is tomorrow's reality. In an important sense, what Bennett proposes is only a different way of talking about the same crude deathly realities that founded this republic. Slavery, racial apartheid, genocide, eugenics, extermination, and disposability have consistently laced the moral language of this nation relative to the black subject, vaguely citizen. And as black history surely reminds all, herein is the frightening underside of America's minority body politic.[107]

The "Negro Problem"

Long in the conservative tradition has that overused "Negro Problem" been ritualistically summoned as the cause of America's declining moral values. Bennett has deviated little from tried and true past practices. In his twenty-first century adaptation, he links a prerequisite for crime reduction to the necessary implementation of a program of eugenics to eliminate the nation's less desirable citizens—in this case, aborting black babies.[108] His controversial words, in effect, advocated for "killing them in the womb," before they can reach the teen years or young adulthood. Polemics such as these, as effectively utilized by Bennett and others, insinuate that young African American males are exclusively to blame for their own problems, as well as for the problems of society at large. Bortner and Williams, authors of *Youth In Prison* dispute that generally accepted wisdom to assert that the real danger in such ideological polemics is that they vilify imprisoned youth for political ends:

The characterization of imprisoned youths as predatory and beyond hope serves symbolic and political ends, especially in reassuring the public that the cause of social unrest has been identified and that politicians and government have taken action to provide safety and maintain social control.[109]

What Bennett's mindset accomplishes is to exaggerate fears that black manchildren are inherently more violent and dangerous; therefore, they must be driven out of the community and condemned to a caged existence. Yesterday, it was the battle cry for prisons and more prisons to cage America's dark "fiends." Today, it is "abort black babies." For young black males, this casual talk of genocide only reacts to amplify fears about their risky state of disposability in a nation unwilling to tolerate their existence outside of death or incarceration.

Taken a step further, this call to "abort black babies" judges young black males as morally and socially inferior. (Defective is how the language was historically applied to the black race.) Such a status is tantamount to their being condemned as social "misfits," with an inherent "weakness" in their moral genetics. Bennett's reasoning seems to draw unerringly from biblical literalists' charge of black people being the so-called "cursed children of Ham." In his opinion, for society to escape the wrath of their "irascible" nature, manchildren's existence must be condemned as defective, thus requiring death as the most expedient remedy to protect the "safety" of an allegedly innocent society.

In everyday terms, when such inflamed moralizing gets applied to manchildren, supposedly they "don't feel any remorse" when they hurt other people. This could explain why Rodney King was called everything and anything but a child of God. I think a gorilla to be exact. Chris Garner of Kirkwood High School decries the fact that "statistics make black teenagers out as the monsters of society…. My friends aren't monsters; they aren't [the] bad [seed]. They're not the ones raping and robbing…. I just don't understand what I see in the media, that all black people are bad."[110] What teen Garner references is that when violence is posed in the language of natural selection, this genetically predetermines manchildren as innately lacking in "compassionate" human qualities and reduces them to the level of "snarling" beasts, bred like wolf packs. Certainly in the media, the virulence of that perception, if not portrayal, holds court among the American public to accuse black youth before they ever step foot in a courtroom. That mentality festers at the very core of the super-predator label, with which many are unfairly burdened. Thus so, manchildren from the inner-city, the more conservative argue, are bred by a "culture of poverty"[111] or manifest "traits" of moral poverty. Either way, the consensus is that they are poverty-stricken at some fundamental human level.

Noticeably, such compromising language pinned onto the very nature and bodies of black youth to condemn them to nonexistence is sensitively reformed for white youth's criminality; so they don't appear as anti-social and predatory. No, not "thugs" produced by "moral poverty"[112] or a "culture of poverty," they are simply copy-cat "wannabes." When white youth drug, commit crimes and murder, "they are not hardened criminals," according to a police official who spoke of a grisly murder committed by three suburban youth, who sealed their crime with a tragic suicide pact. Their deaths were the deadly repercussion of a drug deal gone awry. "They were just kids. They called themselves the D-Mac Crew, a 'gang' of about five or six teenagers… 'wannabees,' small-time youths trying to recreate a video version of a thug's life."[113] Always redemptive, forgiving language is commended to console white youth's deaths as not so nihilistic and thuggish, when compassion should apply to all youth's unnatural deaths, regardless of race. Some boys are blessed with so much grace—white skinned privileged, that is—and others are begrudged even a drop of anointing, when love and mercy are in such a short supply for black boys' lives.

By the same token, ideologues like Bennett are careful not to call attention to the socioeconomic conditions besieging the black community at an alarming rate, such as the failed school system that underserves black children, the high-risk neighborhoods where they grow up, the racial bias in the criminal justice system. Let's not forget the proliferation of handguns, for which gun manufacturers refuse to take responsibility and which fuel angry gang activity. Consider the drug trade that infests the black community to the extent that even a drug czar like Bennett himself was unable to halt its lethal flow. Finally, joblessness and severe public-sector budget cuts began in the early 80s are denied their critical role in intensifying conditions linked to high crime indices.[114] Taken altogether, such travailing social impediments truncate the life chances of young black males—a fact which protectionists like Bennett can conveniently turn a blind eye to refuse their merit in diminishing the manchildren's quality of life and severely limiting their access to mainstream opportunities.

Racism and Crime

The point to make here, sooner than receiving Bennett's rhetoric as innocuous speech, harmless in its effect, it might be more meaningful to assess it critically as the product of an underlying neo-fascist current running throughout conservative right-wing politics in this nation today. Bennett's rhetoric was not voiced in isolation, apart from the regressive milieu that ceded to legitimate his planting seeds of fear and panic in the public mind. A seasoned piece in the 2000 *New Jersey Law Journal*, written by Roger Clegg, President and General Counsel of the Center for Equal Opportunity, titled "Race and Crime," had already hallowed Bennett's bald move: "Since blacks are more likely to be poor and unemployed, then it follows that they will, in the aggregate, commit more crimes."[115] Critics accused Clegg, as they did Bennett, of only "feeding stereotypes" that do little to contribute anything substantial to the debate about the overrepresentation of African Americans in prison. Even before then, in the early 1990s to be exact, Bennett collaborated with contemporaries like John Diulio[116] in *Body Count*, to articulate their harsh moral judgment of (black) juvenile crime and proposed stern solutions. All in that particular neoconservative camp coalesced around this one social consensus: "Young black males commit crime at higher rates than do young white males."[117]

Bennett had long been committed to the theory of the emergence of a juvenile "super-predator"[118] caste of feral young black males, born without the buffers of civil society, families, and churches in urban America. In his book, his code words, "young urban minority males" were his way of signaling black youth. What Bennett was actually trying to signify in indirect terms was gangs. But seemingly his highly inflammatory signification has been indiscriminately applied to all young black males, delinquents or not. This pejorative identity pinned upon young black males proposes to put them all at-risk for criminal suspicion.

In backlash, his book performs a singular purpose, that is, to counter what he considers "liberal" excesses in aiding the state of moral decline in black urban communities by justifying the lack of personal responsibility. On top of castigating liberal excuses, his other mission is to reframe young black male delinquency in the racially charged language of moral poverty and lack of personal responsibility to conceal the derelict role of government accountability. To put in perspective this unbridled demonization of black youth, one critic had this to say about the malicious profiling: "With the kind of so-called Republican moralism, our finest elected officials have not been able to stand the test of integrity with all of their advantages in life. And yet, black youth must pay dearly for sins that have never amounted to the corruption of a nation."[119]

In his moral myopia, Bennett does not consider that society has a role in the humanizing of its people; for him that's solely in the purview of the home. His adoption of this polemic perspective was to the point that in *Body Count*, he argued furiously that the nation's drug and crime problems were fueled largely by moral poverty, a lapsed condition integral to the home environment. Economic poverty, lack of government-funded social programs, racism[120]—he scorned those as the same old "liberal" litany for excusing any and everything gone wrong with black America since the "liberal" sixties. When it comes to defending black youth delinquency, those long-adopted excuses, as he opines, suffer from lost moral currency.

Unflinching in his conservative view of the role of government, Bennett subordinates its accountability to the life of the home and "religious faith." And only when those social institutions fail must the state step in to apprehend the violator and punish him to the fullest extent of the law. Rehabilitation sends the wrong message, as Bennett surmises. "People are frustrated because government is failing to carry out its first and most basic responsibility: to provide for the security of its citizens in order to meet the promise of liberty and justice for all."[121] Bennett pleads for security over protection of civil liberties, at all costs. A police or national security state is the primary function of government in his mind to the exclusion of providing a safety net for the protection of its most vulnerable citizens. Never acknowledged was the role of the state in exacerbating conditions that led to a kind of social determinism currently operating in the lives of black youth.

Bennett's position does beg the question: if the root causes of moral poverty are inextricably linked to "out-of-wedlock" births and their related condition of economic poverty negatively impacting a generation of black youth, how does he explain more drug use in white homes? How does he explain the so-called "moral poverty" of white children who are of two parent families, living in the suburbs? For their moral misdeeds, is that blame, too, laid at the feet of black youth? If so, then black youth are a powerful mighty force which this nation has yet to reckon with; nor have these young men touched the collective power of their own strength.

What was particularly surprising in the book is that Bennett's nostalgic moral imagination consistently harped back to the days when white America was safe, "niggers" knew their place, and there was, of course, not this rabid moral failing weakening an American superpower infrastructure in the world. In all actuality, controlling that moral weak link was exactly what his book was committed to doing under the guise of evangelizing America to take action before its internal moral failure becomes an Alcatraz. Bennett's unreasonable yearning for back then, when crime was "down," cherishes a social climate quite adverse to black life in his "good 'ole" days. How crime was being counted and even acknowledged as a crime is something to consider. How many lynchings went into the official record? In the "good 'ole" days the rape of a black woman couldn't be prosecuted as a crime, if the rapist was a white man.[122] In *Body Count*, his statistics are inundated with crimes of rape and murder to convince America just how widespread crime really is, and therefore our moral failing. In preparation for the global wars, Bennett is of the mindset that America needs to shed its weakest link. That's social Darwinism at its level best. Not just some absentminded chatter, his "abort black babies" public policy solution can be placed into its sinister context. What Bennett fails to comprehend is that without help to the bleeding humanity right at her doorstep this country will implode from within. America will not have to wait for the global forces to disembowel her superpower status.

Bennett shies away from the obvious, though. For example, why are there so many guns set loose on urban streets? It is a subject hidden under the cover of shining a light on the moral degeneracy of young black males. From the shocking reports of the daily news, the public knows guns are in the hands of young people, murderous on college campuses, terrorizing high school classrooms, and deadly in urban drive-by's. Regrettably though, Bennett doesn't see guns as the common denominator in these homicides and related crimes. When weapons of mass death are placed in children's hands, expect irresponsible use. Get the glut of unregulated guns off the street, pass laws on gun control, and see how it turns this situation around, is what I propose.

From what's already been said, high-profile personalities like Bennett, with their ideological posturing, are adept in producing mass justification and acceptance for the disposability of young black males. That is the unfailing function of ideology in a well-oiled hegemony: to present the extreme as transparent truth, without question. The supposed transparency of such propaganda sets up the public sentiment to readily accept what history would condemn as unacceptable. For instance, mass murder throughout history, one of those grisly obituaries, confronts us with the inevitable fact that any ideology associated with extremism is always dangerous to the well-being of marginal citizens or resented peoples. It is quite akin to that dark western history of fascist extermination. In a moment, any targeted prey can morph into a national scapegoat to "solve" a politicized socioeconomic or "crime" problem; or its identity can be puppeted by the reigning power-that-be as "the blame" or the necessary blood-letting "solution" to create a perception of national stability. In calling for the "aborting of black babies," Bennett tactically stroked that anxiety of fear ever smoldering in white imagination as a catalyst to mobilize a stance of protectionism within the American polis against those ever made the racial other, of those whose very black embodiment resists assimilation as a valued melting pot citizen. The inevitable outcome of construing such a fear condones the necessity of black sacrifice and suffering as the scapegoat appeasement for the sake of restoring national favor, stability and prosperity.[123] Bennett's call is for the American public to react from their unthinking emotions. (Whereas this liberal public may sanction black disposability, everyone should be asking the question, who's next? In whose backyard will the moral scapegoating end, if ever? Sweet Honey in the Rock, an activist African American female *a cappella* ensemble, sings a haunting song, "When They Come For Me.") Blacks condemned Bennett's racist speech as an alternative kind of lynch politics being vetted in "respectable" white conservative circles.

The Nooses of Jena

Countering Bennett's conservative, lopsided argument, according to the work of respected sociologist William J. Wilson, joblessness trumps as the critical element in the downward spiral taking urban communities by storm. He writes, "Many of today's problems in the inner-city ghetto neighborhoods—crime, family dissolution, welfare, low levels of social organization, and so on—are fundamentally a consequence of the disappearance of work."[124] In shifting jobs to the suburbs with little public transportation from the inner-cities or just outright shipping jobs abroad, joblessness factors as critical in aggravating conditions of family destabilization, homelessness, neighborhood blight, and worsening drug and alcohol problems. The rapacious forces of neoliberalism or globalization, in full swing, account for gutting the U.S. industrial sector to place enormous strain on the domestic economy.[125] In pandering to corporate America at the expense of abandoning its own workers, the U.S. government has been least helpful in this global economic transition. How could our government have assumed that the shift in the industrial sector in the U.S. economy would make little difference in the lives of real people, especially to those semi-skilled and unskilled workers who depended on those high-wage union jobs? As one baby boomer complained, "My father was supposed to bring me into the factory. All I had to do was perfect a skill on the assembly line, and could expect to retire with a livable pension. Not so any longer. Those jobs are all gone now." These workers in distress come from the white and black working-classes. So it would seem that in the midst of this economic downsizing, it's not just black folks crying the blues; the blues has also taken residence in white working-class neighborhoods as well. Black people understand that something is afoot in working-class white America, when there is this prowling for scapegoats to demonstrate the class dissatisfaction with the "good 'ole" American way. And when white working-class America is up in arms, it's sure to spell trouble for black folks, and could stir up old traumas of terror for black children.

Let's not forget in this nation's history, nooses have always been the weapon of vigilante racial fear.

With some whites' noose-ready response in overdrive over their anxiety and fear of threatening economic collapse, borne out most frighteningly in widespread mortgage foreclosure and a Great Depression scare right around the corner, I wonder whom Bennett would be more interested in protecting or blaming? Historically, in times of national economic hardships with their accompanying problems, it's been a longstanding tradition to return to what is tried and true, that is, blaming the "niggers" rather than the causes of the economic trauma. The U.S. government has much to answer for in its commitment to facilitating the free reign of an avaricious global market over the protection of its vulnerable citizens, i.e. aiding and abetting job flight to fund corporate globalization. Even Bennett has relied upon what has always been a foolproof tactic of a racist society in economic crisis—playing the race card. What some of this surely articulates is that, as liberal as America would like to posture herself after the gains of the sixties, still a frightening undertow of dark behavior plagues this nation's survival instinct, to the point of it being noose-ready to pounce upon any perceived or real threat of economic competition, usually drawn along racially defined lines. Yes, the Jena 6 case has been the most politicized and high-profile, but this isn't just about the South or Jena, Louisiana. Nooses are showing up all over New York, at Columbia Teacher's College, at the MTA worksite, on blue-collar jobs all over New York. It's about a climate of fear that disregards civil liberties protection best modeled by the rogue behavior of the Bush's White House;[9] it conspires to threaten all based upon race, class, and gender inequities. In this economic scenario, really the nooses are directed at all of America's "others." And although immigrants would want to cherish an America dream pure and pristine, divorced from its sordid past that's paraded in the faces and skin of those made the other, the "nigger," the foreigner—such as the Amerindians, blacks, the Chinese, and every immigrant group that bore its racial wrath—that self-deception, though bought into, cannot persist, which is, that America's brutal history of extremist race relations has passed and only its golden age awaits. That self-deception is contested by the likes of a Jena 6. In my mind, Jena 6 is a test case about whether conditions are ripe for a return of white supremacy rule with its tradition of terrorist fear in pockets of America's economy, including corporate policies and practices as well as various public institutions.

Back to Bennett's highly suspect and polemical reasoning, at best, it is premised precipitously on a faulty rationale that if the people who do the crime are eliminated, crime will melt away. Yet, even with the falling violent crime rates among young black males,[127] he does little to explain why incarceration among them remains at an unprecedented high. His extreme sentiments and their impact in the public domain conspire with socioeconomic factors to perpetuate the criminalization and incarceration of young black males and that growing population of black women, who will spend a significant portion of their lives behind prison bars. Public policy analyst John Flateau places the blame elsewhere, rather than on that vulnerable societal scapegoat, the beleaguered young black male:

> The prison industrial complex has become by result, if not by intent, an institutionally racist tool of destruction, tacitly sanctioned by the tyranny and silence of the majority. It is overwhelmingly and effectively neutralizing young Black and Latino American males. The outcomes spell devastation for Black and Latino communities....[128]

Race Matters

The fact is, society has had an ongoing affair with the young black male's demonization. If perception is the reality, the American white public harbors an unfounded fear of black youth, regardless of the criminal data to the contrary that bear out most crimes are intraracial rather than interracial. Yet white citizens believe that at any given moment they might fall prey to a "big" threatening black criminal element. That bone-chilling perception of manchildren jeopardizes their chances of survival in a world that already relishes an ancient and unreasonable fear of blackness, without apology, religiously so. Such perceptions have been charged with engineering a world order antagonistic to all of black embodiment.

In *The Angela Y. Davis Reader,* political abolitionist and theorist Angela Davis, forceful in her analysis, posits that "race matters inform, more than ever, the ideological and material structures of U.S. society."[129] From what Davis proposes, it would be fair to say that Bennett's ideological biases tapped into that ever-operative fear which plagues white citizens regarding the very embodiment of blackness—whether in its sexual or economic incarnation. Ever-present at some subliminal level, this fear shares the responsibility for the conflation of the terms "blackness" and "crime" in the public mind, thus making possible the extreme suggestion of a public policy solution, as earnestly advocated by Bennett before he retracted his position. Apparently his frustration was directed at the "inability" of the criminal justice system to do more in locking up all black youth; so his recommendation is for the government to take matters into its our own hands and just kill them in the womb, as a matter of public policy. For once and for all, society will be rid of its "moral pest." On the flip side of Bennett's remarks, though, he tried to make light of them. But, in the final analysis, his position on "abort black babies" outs the open secret of the Right-to-Life Movement—a movement he's sure to support, given his affiliation with the Heritage Foundation. That is, it does not value every life at conception, only those threatened white fetuses. There is much hypocrisy that breaks down along racial lines in the Right-to-Life Movement.

Finally, Davis stabs at the heart of the matter. She posits that no matter how much color-blind rhetoric is espoused by American policy-makers, fear operates as an integral component of white racism. In the case of the two-tiered criminal justice system, ominously tilted against black males, that fear influences how public policy is written and enforced with lethal consequences relative to the life chances of young black males. [130] According to Davis, one of the grim realities, which affects all Americans, is that the "naturalization of black people as criminals thus also erects ideological barriers to an understanding of the connections between late twentieth-century structural racism and the globalization of capital."[131] Placed within this stark context, young black males are constrained to resist on two fronts: the furious advancement of global corporate capitalism and the ominous establishment of the national security state, which feeds the prison industrial complex pipeline their life blood.

Regarding the life chances of black youth, this collusion of social, economic, and political fortune targets black male youth disproportionately for disposability and undercuts their ability, quite frankly, to function as valued citizens.

CHAPTER 4

Black Masculinity
Of Masters and Men

My biggest cry is for us to really reflect on who we are…. Who are we in our manhood? Who are we in our responsibility to the black woman and the black child?

Entertainer Bill Cosby

We are in desperate need again of responsible, in-house, adult Black males—men who infuse their charges, by example, with positive self-images and value systems; men who will teach young men how to face life's adversities without resorting to violence; men who will make the time and commitment to show their sons, rather than tell them how to be men; and finally men who are secure enough in their own manhood to understand the difference between fathering and raising a children.

Herbert Dyer, Jr.

If you live in a world controlled by White men, then the greatest threat to Black men would come not from women but from other men. The best way to destroy the Black family is to destroy the Black man.

Jawanza Kunjufu

Striving for manhood in an American world poses an irreconcilable dilemma for young black males.[132] It always has for black men. Then, from the start, masculinity begs the question of what manhood must look like for young native sons in a nation with its long history of being intimidated by the racial embodiment of black masculinity. Much of its irrational angst toward black manhood was spawned by America's wishful imagination, sexual politics, and supremacist power. In actual fact, she has deeply feared black manhood at one of its most basic levels of human activity, that is, white fear of black male sexuality.[133] And the cost of that deep fear has exacted precious blood. For instance, from this twisted fear was spun a menacing myth of the black male rapist, to which countless black males forfeited their castrated lives. Still, the noose and the lynch tree signify the blood altar where this deadly mob subordination ritual was brazenly enacted on cursed black bounty as a triumphant public spectacle. And to this very day, those profane blood-scarred symbols invoke the most visceral reaction to America's control of black manhood.[134] Subsequently, it can't be said forcefully enough, black manhood has never been trouble-free in a society that has only deeded the right to experience its preferential notions to white men and penalized the racial outsiders for any hint of trespassing. With its punishment, swift and deadly, manchild Emmit Till's lynching was one of its lethal historical tragedies. In an earlier period, the Jena 6[135] would have suffered a similar necktie fate, all inextricably tied to a fetish fear of black masculinity. In today's court of public opinion, barring that former vigilante freedom to seek the tallest tree, incarceration offers a second best option to contain black masculinity. Notwithstanding the hostile nature of this society's ambivalence toward black manhood, herein is exactly where the manchild hunts for his masculine identity. When considering an at-risk community that resides within a well-controlled white male racial order, the serious weight given to the nature of this socially prescribed reality of manhood is no small matter for each generation of black sons. To that extent, critical issues pertinent to informing, defining and restricting young black masculine identity will be persistently pursued throughout this essay to aid in the manchild's quest toward young adulthood.

Nobody Knows My Name: "Boy"

In point of fact, that mister/Mr. social title prefacing black males' surnames can only loom large as a false symbol of social yearning, taunting their fervent stride toward an unreachable manhood. Yet it has always been a respectful title deferentially reserved for those whom black males call "The

Man," once Master. "Boy" was the highest that colored manhood could ever rise in white society's eye. His demoralization spills over into race relations today, orienting society to deficit notions of black male humanity. Spat out from history past, "boy" browbeat black men into daily submission to a domesticated status of black male inferiority. It aimed to threaten and subdue the black community's manhood into timid subordination. Brandished about as a master's weapon of razor-sharp demoralization, "boy" was spitefully employed to create a debilitating anxiety about just who the black male was in relation to his maligned identity and oppressed community. The self-doubts raised were meant to weaken his ability to resist white male power at all, as it haughtily raped and pillaged the black community. The overall intent struck a fatal death blow against every evidence of threatening black manhood; for, a meek, docile "boy" could never be mistaken for "uppity," headstrong black manhood in a pre-sixties' world. Whether it always achieved it nefarious end or not, as a choice derogatory affixed to every black male, "boy" was to tame any "unlawful" soul uprising within the black male for his true Kunte Kinte identity, until elderly enough to graduate into the highest a black man could hope to attain in white eyes—a mild-mannered uncle. Even today, tutored from decades past black manhood has been doomed as America's perpetual whipping "boy."

Could this explain why in the latter half of the twentieth century that the American public has had an insatiable obsession with underdeveloped, infantilized black male characters like child stars Emmanuel Lewis in *Webster* (1983), Bryton McClure as Little Richie in *Family Matters* (1989), or Gary Coleman as Arnold in *Diff'rent Strokes* (1978)? Typecast as miniature public pets never human souls, the media fantasy prefers that manchildren never mature into responsible, young adults or full-grown adult men. What kind of double message does that send to young black males? [136] As soon as they mature into black male youth, they lose human currency. Stay a "boy-child" is the warning from a hostile society, if not in body image, then in attitude. In its preference for a non-threatening, docile, infantilized black male or "boy," white fears reproduce their own fantasy of what black manhood should resemble in order to cope within their own threshold of racial angst. And so has been the case historically for the black male, who has always been the projection of America's worst and deepest fears, before ever performing an act to justify his shackling, his lynching, his death to calm her irrational anxiety. The same applies to the vigorous incarceration of black manchildren. The difficulty for them is that, even before young adulthood, they are already profiled as targets of white fear and quickly vilified in the mass media as an uncontainable threat to law-and-order. Their youthful identity is politicized as a super-predator, cast as an "unleashed" Michael Vick on the hunt to inflict injury on more than blood-thirsty canines, but upon a so-called benevolent American public and its valued trophies. This projection of fear, partial to a white fantasy, carries disastrous consequences for black youth's grasp for manhood in a race-driven world.

Up to the present, "boy" has lost none of its social luster. Recently acquainted with a newly injured Equal Employment Opportunity (EEO) tale confirms suspicions of its indomitable career. A black woman was asked to participate in a straw interview, really because of her race; the candidate who her boss happened to be interviewing was a young black male candidate. After the interview her boss assured her with a casual indifference: "That 'boy' wouldn't be a good candidate because he doesn't have enough experience." He took refuge in that that dutiful "not qualified," which bars black males excessively from opportunities in institutional structures. But lacking any real power to influence a choice in the interview proceedings, she was called upon to be an institutional collaborator. Although mob vigilantism has been reformed from wreaking its deadly blood sentences, an institutional culture of hostility and exclusion yet prevails against black manhood. In all of this, she understood that that "boy" characterization did something detrimental in a culture of black male belittlement: its claim of "not qualified" refused him an able and experienced manhood. Voicing her stance of solidarity in an uncertain dissent, She said: "He's not a boy, that's a man." With white power on his side, her boss feigned a racial amnesia that denies any historical precedence to suggest his chauvinistic language as racially charged and inappropriate. Such fresh blood narratives strung-up everyday are readily dismissed with "I didn't mean anything by it"; in other words, this is how racial ignorance is left cocooned in its own ill-spirited complacency, unbothered. Ever so politely, it awaits a new day for its harmful indiscretion. And, of course, the "boy" didn't get the job.

Hidden in polite on-the-job politics, in some of the most likely places of EEO enforcement, is where master and mistress prejudices thrive as forms of racial terrorism in the lives of modern-day African American men. Even to this present day, economic, political, and social barriers racially align themselves to stall black males' social progress in a race-addicted society. Though much of racism's blatant crudeness has been legally reformed, veiled and made subtler today by the palatable proclamations of EEO and affirmative action progress, yet white majority preferences and privileges still rule the roost with racial exclusion and discrimination, marking black existence as late as the twenty-first century. The pervasiveness of racial exclusion is measured not only in how black males are "…being affected by individual and group racism," but also "affected by institutionalized racism, which in fact can have longer-term and more damaging effects."[137] These systemic discriminatory practices very much integral to the culture of institutional racism were reported on by a CNN special. Basically, the report said that companies in the US would rather hire a white man with a felony record and no high school education before they would hire a black man with no criminal record and a 4-year degree.[138] This institutional twist on a present-day Jim Crow "separate but equal" has rendered black males almost invisible in the mainstream of American life to the extent of them being nearly impotent in resisting a socially fated exclusion.

Of keen interest though, before leaving this important section, is how a social perversion has made men boys and boys men in the black community. This social paradox is borne out most acutely in the criminal justice system. Though children in the eyes of the law, manchildren are regularly tried as adults.

This perversion of justice is rooted in a troubling history in the black community, dating back to when black boys were tried as men by lynch mobs. Fourteen-years-old Emmitt Till received an adult execution. Manchildren, tried as adults, have hit an all time high low for juvenile offenders. A growing trend, specific to the criminal justice system, is how manchildren are being cast as responsible, mature adults who can accept the consequences for their delinquent actions, rather than as misguided youth in need of adult counsel. "Nationwide, young black offenders are more than twice as likely to be transferred to adult court as their white counterparts."[139] Stooping past fifteen-and sixteen-year-olds, the system currently tries and sentences twelve-year olds. For instance, twelve-years-old Lionel Tate of Miami, Florida was the first, youngest youth convicted in US history in 2001 as an adult. Getting younger and younger, black youth are being transferred to adult courts for prosecution on a daily basis.[140] That strategic move of conferring adult status on black youth for purposes of criminalization advocates only to incarcerate black youth at surreal numbers. But how does the black community reconcile this duality of "boy" and adult abiding together in the bodies of black youth and in the confused mind of a punitive state, uncommitted to sustaining poor, black manchildren?

From the perspective of these vulnerable manchildren, our nation's investment in their criminalization and incarceration saddles them with a long-term handicap that keeps them perpetual boys: disenfranchised of voting rights, inability to get and hold a job, much less a decent wage earning job— little to nil family support for their children, or even the emotional capital necessary to sustain a loving adult relationship.[141] Then, there is the inevitable likelihood of homelessness, a growing synonym for being black, single, male, and obsolete in America. With this nation's race to incarcerate black males, they fall back once again into a culture of belittlement as "boys" of the state, placed under "adult" corrections supervision. These adversarial conditions destine them ever to be dependent children, boys, in adult bodies.

Lastly, with its deeply soiled history, "boy" feeds the contempt that this society holds for black boys and men, cursing them into disposability. Daily, the toxic legacy of this consummate racial powerbroker, "boy," undermines black men's longing to stand up and be counted as men, and to teach their sons how to be a man. A relic since before the sixties still grips America's racial imagination, and thrives in the social fabric of a twenty-first century post-civil rights world.

On the Death of the "N-Word"

That libelous "n-word" requires expanding on within the parallel social context of "boy," for both are inextricably debilitating, dehumanizing, and threatening in a history-sensitive, black imagination. Indeed, traversing that blasphemous distance between "boy" and the "n-word" is really quite short indeed in white America's mind and black people's moral imagination, too. In today's racial context, though one hears less of that social taunt, boy, it's still alive and well in the cultural pool of racial expletives, etiquette, and attitude. And its social injury is not dead and buried in black cultural imagination. For the "n-word" carries as much social baggage as "boy" and does the same libelous duty in the racial imagination, if not worse; rightfully black people should not seek its redemption, but satisfactory burial, despite naysayers' protest of its subversive and unifying power. (Yes, I am aware that it is vociferously protested that the "n-word" has different connotations for different communities, depending upon age, race, community, class, and social setting.) At-large and on the prowl, still, the "n-word" is crucifying new victims. When Mikhail Markhasev shot and killed Ennis William Cosby on January 16, 1997, his bigoted confession to his friends was, "I shot a nigger. It's all over the news."[142] His use of the "n-word" was lethally aimed to invoke the withering depth of contempt he felt for black people. It boasts his new idolatrous standing as a *bona fide* American racist—true blue. "I'm one of you now," bragged his racial bonding. And he just a recent immigrant, what are the benefits to long-term citizens?

Although in its present day evolution, the n-word has traded in its abusive history-making "er" signifier to benefit from a boisterous hip hop facelift, replaced with a so-called innocuous "a" attached to the end versus the standard "er." The newer version, more inclusive, I guess, makes everybody a "nigga" now or so it seems. Supposedly, the hurt souls of black folks are all but redeemed with a slight elision as if it could exorcize centuries-old indignities from a racially sordid racial past. For those who suffered the everyday, public insults and injuries to their manhood by the "n-word," it has yet to endure a proper burial. (Driving a stake through the heart of a ghost is never an easy kill.)

Enjoying a civil-rights distance from its cruel soul lacerations, rejecting the burden of its racial past, this generation of hip hop brothers celebrate "you my nigga" as a proud badge of affection and honor, which they bestow generously upon one another and their white comrades. Who can fault the hip hop generation for feeling honor-bound to protect themselves from the past eviscerating damages of the "n-word" by widening the racial field of the "n-word" influence? If adopted by all, unlike their parents' generation, they could escape the wrenching wrath of its soul degradation; their humanity left uncrucified by this consummate racial powerbroker if it attained a liberal social use. When wielded against them, it wouldn't wound the same, was what they hoped in their crossover innocence. Their social and psychological maneuvering proposed to present a cunning twist on that once "separate but equal" identity: in our human baseness, we are all "nigga" equal, rather than in our inherent value as children of God. But how successful the crossover appeal has been in truly inverting the humiliation of the "n-word" into an innocuous epithet leaves grave doubts. Time will tell in race relation. But in the black community, for sure, as much as I hear advocates defending black youth in their liberal wielding of "nigga" in their hip hop lingo, I have never heard it spat out most contemptuously to hurt one another's black humanity in "yeah, you, my nigga," aimed as an angry ballistic to slay one another into a homicidal death. Alive and well, its animus of spirit murder has not been tamed, in my opinion. Nor has the "nigga" fraternity rescinded in any measurable manner the homicidal statistics menacing black youth. They seems to corroborate just how meaningless they still believe their lives are.[143]

Will the National Association for the Advancement of Colored People (NAACP) symbolic burial of the "n-word" have any discernible dent in fostering language that values black brotherhood and their right to an unharassed life? Or is the social angst that spawned the bastardry use of this term so deeply soiled by its tainted past that even more drastic steps must be taken to abolish its hold on the black and white moral imagination?[144] What will emancipate our youth from its persuasive social seduction? In effect, the "n-word" survival's speaks to some of the powerlessness of the African American community to control what disparages black identity.

From the other side, regardless of how much white youth might clamor to attach themselves to this "term of endearment," "nigga," as a genuine show of favor in their being "down with it" and "real" in their idolatrous infatuation with hip hop culture, that term has never been pilfered by or applied to white manhood.

Trials of Black Manhood

Protest literature written over the past centuries from the conscientious objections of abolitionist martyr David Walker in his fiery *Appeals*[145] to the blood-scorching speeches of freedom fighter Malcolm X, hammers the point exhaustively that black men generally, and strong black men in particular, were and still are regarded as the enemy within U.S. society. (That could explain why so many are locked up.) Those who refused that cherished American race tradition of servile obedience and rejected assimilation into its supremacist world view paid dearly, usually with their broken lives. Those who stood up by questioning its legitimacy, its authority, suffered the unbridled wrath of this nation's white fury. Weapons of tyranny, employed against black manhood to tame it into compliance by any means necessary, boast government collusion in every possible way imaginable of an imperialist state, from the flagrant abuses of the coercive power of the IRS, to the red-hunt of Macarthyism, the unpoliced vigilante zeal of lynch mobs, to FBI snooping and incrimination, and political assassinations, among the many. Indeed, there is an endless list of those who bore the bloody cross of the hate crimes of this nation's breaking conditions. But who can forget the besmirching of Paul Robeson with a communist stain; the government harassment of W.E.B. Dubois until he finally fled this country for the promised land of Ghana, the violent assassination of that non-violent civil rights sentinel, Dr. King, who transformed America with a justice-seeking dream; the outright murder of Panther Fred Hampton—who only promised to "love the people and to die for the people,"; the mocking of Reverend Jesse Jackson's rainbow leadership by former President Clinton in his caricature of the 2008 presidential primary campaign of Barack Obama with the jeer, "Even Jesse Jackson won South Carolina"; and the Justice Department's scare tactic in investigating civil right activist Reverend Al Sharpton. This litany only invokes a few names of courageous black men who were put to the martyr's fires of death and defeat. Some died, but many survived as unfading symbols of race hope and stubborn pride and resistance.

Indeed, the reign of racial terror within the African American context is nothing new. Its roots are as deep as the birth of this confederacy itself. Black history long remembers the days of the violent rituals of "breaking" incorrigible slaves like Frederick Douglass. Just as pernicious, but less volatile, although equally injurious to human dignity and pride, the traditional down cast eyes or the degrading "bowin'" and "scratchin'" and "yes'suh" mannerisms mimicked the breaking or obedience rituals enforced upon segregated Negroes. This carefully choreographed dance of subordination, impeccably maneuvered with the possible risk of black death for any accused slip-ups, reinforced the supremacist hierarchy of race relations. It also acquired Oscar-winning applause, in Morgan Freeman, as the character Hoke, portraying that tamed docility in the 1990 film, *Driving Miss Daisy*.[146] But in Hollywood's preoccupation, if not arrogance, to image the "bowin'" and "scratchin'" insipidly right, it missed the finer nuances of black history's resistance: "We wear the mask that grins and lies/ It hides our cheeks and shades our eyes."[147] Black men "bowin'" and "scratchin'," especially in places without an anxious itch, "skinnin'" and "grinnin'" when the joke was on them—some blacks called it "cheezin'," and that, not so long ago—pacified a white master authority of black total subordination. Yes, simulating that subordination tradition was much like Morgan Freeman's "yes'suh" and "ma'amming" Miss Daisy (Jessica Tandy) in every other breath to appease her anxiety that handy Hoke only wanted to shuffle in his dutiful, deferential place. Along similar lines of black male emasculation come these particular queries: I wonder if that was former President Bill Clinton's problem with Senator Obama in those 2008 primaries? Was it Obama's unclipped manhood? To choose to be free, human, and equal was that what Clinton seemed to resent? Oddly, Obama was called an elitist by Senators John McCain and Hillary Clinton. Was that a polite way of calling him an "uppity nigger'" At any rate, such familiar disciplines of male subordination attained their projected aim of mocking the black community's striving for strong black manhood. For any "arrogant" notion of a strong black man hastily received subjugation in a white imagination as an "uppity" hyperbole that suffers most from vain desire than an ounce of reality. In a supremacist mindset, black identity must ever emulate its original condition, that deferential humanity of a slave or else threaten a master's identity.

This brief quote sums up well the pre-sixties' attack upon black masculinity that retains strong elements of that domesticating behavior today in race relations: "The centerpiece of white supremacy is disrespect and servile obedience. A byproduct is apartheid."[148] Instances of this subordination mindset are problematically evident today in black males' encounter with law enforcement officers. Regardless of who they are, in such encounters, black males from every walk of life, professionals and non-professionals, must adopt a docile posture to represent themselves as of no threat—tamed, in a word; otherwise, they are treated as a menacing Rodney King or death-dealing Sean Bell. Gun or no gun present isn't the issue; being black, free and male is grounds for an unmerited execution.

Today, youth of the hip hop generation, impatient with that ingratiating social jig from ages past and its troubling resurgence today, imposed upon the black community by penalty of black male death, refuse its social authority to control their adopting any domesticating behavior that they deem as "disrespectful." Their brash swagger bears repeating: "I am very much like a lot of heads in the hip hop generation. I am not going to smile, shuffle, or give a good g—damn what anyone thinks about me, and that most assuredly includes White folks."[149] Their proud attitude rejects that servile etiquette of Ellison's invisible man, once reserved for masters and slaves. Unwilling to constantly apologize for their social existence, their downright attitude acquires prominence in their politically laden rap lyrics. As Public Enemy raps: "The minute they see me, fear me/ I'm the epitome - a public enemy/ Used, abused without clues/ I refused to blow a fuse/ They even had it on the news/ Don't believe the hype...." Lost to elder generations before them, hip hop brothers are on a mission to settle the score and seize their rightful due, "respect," without permission or apology. In their eyes, it is seen as the only currency to broker in the marketplace of black and white manhood. On the flip side, their public brazenness is misconstrued as giving officers "attitude," and sets them apart as "public enemy" number one, making them a much sought-after trophy of police profiling.

"I Am A Man"

Given how this society has actively administered death threat and lynch campaigns to intimidate black males from escorting dominant, respected notions of manhood, could explain why during the 1960s, black males pursued a relentless campaign to assert that ever elusive manhood withheld. And so explains why that exact sixties' manhood is also under virulent attack today in the mass incarceration of black males throughout this nation.[150] View any 1960s film footage of the civil rights movement. What was boldly affirmed and stamped imprudently on pristine white placards was: "I AM A MAN" or "WE WILL HAVE OUR MANHOOD." Women and men proudly paraded those placards in marches, mass demonstrations, and protest activities, seeking *his* manhood. In his deeply inspirational text, *The Black Messiah*, black nationalist preacher Reverend Cleage interprets just how that 1960s civil disobedience loosened black people's double consciousness from the dutiful tyranny of that white-imposed, servile manhood etiquette. Although not a fan of Dr. King's non-violent philosophy, Cleage candidly evaluates the beneficial aspect from King's strong philosophical stance: "... King had created the confrontation situations in which we began to learn, step by step, that black people can unite, black people can fight, black people can die for the things they believe in." Cleage places the real victory for black people, not in "what white people did; the victory was in how we were changing and in what was happening in our *mind*s" (italics added). His persuasive insight discerns the policing function of imperialism to impose upon an oppressed people an internalized moral vulnerability that coerces individual and group consciousness, in addition to constricting their behavior, to adapt and adjust to the psychological shackles of subjugation. Indeed, if liberation begins as a state of consciousness, it begins in the mind.

Cleage's honest perception notices the fact that also performing notions of strong black manhood on any large scale go directly to the heart of certain movement activities within the black community (and thus the significance of maintaining a grassroots movement for social change as vital). Malcolm X's autobiography speaks affectionately of how proud his father was to affiliate with the Garvey U.N.I.A, for instance.[151] "As young as I was then, I knew from what I overheard that my father was saying something that made him a 'tough' man. I remember an old lady, grinning and saying to my father, 'You're scaring these white folks to death!'" To his dying day, Malcolm

X cherished that proud image of his father crusading in Lansing, Michigan, employing the militant language of the Garvey movement to seize respect for black manhood. Such proud black manhood has been no easy task for black men. It has warranted death for many courageous souls. Malcolm's father was found dead, murdered was his son's long time suspicion, bashed in the head and run over by a streetcar in Lansing, Michigan.[152]
Indeed, from culture to culture, notions of masculinity vary. Its definition within a culture changes over time. As in any culture, masculinity is socially construed to accommodate the moral, social, and political ends of a dominant society, insofar that that society controls the cultural rights to impose its notions of masculinity, sanction them as status quo or normative, and then endow such notions with the power to punish and police those whose behavior strays in transgressing boundaries of what is equated as normally male. Certainly, in the west, and generally, the world defines manhood as protecting and providing for one's family. When not meeting this basic standard, society casts serious doubt upon his masculinity and perceives him as being woefully deficient (i.e. not a man).[153] In America, the social conspiracy against black manhood was especially borne out in the withholding of family wage jobs to black males, in the separation of black men from their families as protectors and guides, and in the social insistence that black men live invisible lives in cages of incarceration. In spite of that traitorous history, to date, black men have borrowed liberally from the white male notion of manhood, particularly as provider, protector, and procreator. However, unlike white men, black males lacked consistent access to similar resources to fulfill the culturally valued vision of masculinity. Over centuries of being harassed by white America's race and gender politics has systematically dispossessed them of accessing many legitimate venues to establish themselves as strong black men, deserving the status and prestige typically conferred upon that male identity.[154] Likewise, from over centuries of black male humiliation and shame, black people should resign themselves to this irrefutable truth: strong masculinity will not come without

a mighty struggle; nor is it a gender power that will be gifted by the largesse of any oppressor. External controls or limitations imposed from the outside, task the black community to develop alternative norms of manhood in service to black survival, accompanied with their affirming rituals and practices. In regards to black manhood, the community must boldly struggle for its definition and its manifestation. One instance of this was fostered at the Million Man March when Minister Farrakhan presented a concept of "manhood" that extended protection and provision to the personal responsibility of inner transformation, as an added characteristic of manhood. As pledged at the Million Man March, "...From this day forward, I will strive to improve myself spiritually, morally, mentally, socially, politically and economically for the benefit of myself, my family and my people." The March itself was a call for atonement, reconciliation, and responsibility.

In short, American society actively withholds "manhood" norms from black men that place them at a distinct disadvantage in integrating into the mainstream of larger society. In the long run it encourages, if not condones, attacks upon their manhood. From a public policy perspective to personal preference, black men are yielded few viable alternatives appropriate to affirming "I am a man" in history and in the eyes of their beloved community. In light of that, some of that highly controversial behavior disparaging black men as irresponsible, and for which they are relentlessly chided by the black community, reflect the moral ambivalence besieging black masculinity today.

Ambivalence Toward Black Mothers and Women

With so much social ambivalence about black mothers rearing black sons, it would be morally negligent not to broach the subject as it pertains to black masculinity. And never more so is the discussion necessary, given that black women are facing an angry tribe of manchildren today, whose scars are still fresh from that boyhood rejection by absentee fathers. Ambivalent about how to feel and whom to hate, one manchild admits blaming his mother: "Silently I began to blame my mother for my father's disappearance.... I grew to hate her and all females, for I felt it was women who made men act as we do."[155] That abusive, misogynist rage some manchildren carry around places all women in jeopardy and makes every woman guilty and subject to the hammer of their clenched fist—the innocent and the guilty alike. And although manchildren know better, but hurt emotionally, those hemorrhaging souls are raging at their absentee fathers for not showing up, for condemning them to that lesser plane of unwanted, for not being there to take the angry weight of their wrath.[156] One hip hop author, Michael Powell, is quite vocal about his own abandonment, as well as this out-of-control absentee dad problem plaguing the black community. Being forsaken by his own father at age seven inflicted a life-size scar upon his own psychic journey to manhood—a soul wound which has required a lifetime for him to recover from, even now, not completely for sure. This could explain why Powell is not the least bit modest about scolding absentee fathers and calling them accountable. Unrelenting in his admonishment, Powell tongue-lashes this broken trust as the "worst form of cowardice, to bring a child into the world and then abandon that child either because you cannot cope or because you and the child's mother are not able to get along." He dares to ask that reproachful question, "How many Black boys and Black girls have had their emotional beings decimated by that father void?"[157] Surely, this could account for some of that simmering rage which churns within manchildren, festering, waiting to be unleashed at the inopportune time upon those closest to them—their mothers, their partners, and their peers. Spewed out in acts of abuse, assault, or with a gunshot blast against what they resent as their unfair life fate, most are not tapped into how that throbbing angst kindles too much of their lethal behavior. Their uncapped rage must be reformed into more positive, life-affirming behavior if this generation is to be rescued.

However, hovering statistics, even more, are frightening in what they allege about the internal conflict between black men and women. Could some of that unhealthy rage manchildren harbor account for detrimental aspects of grown-up black male/female relationship? According to Richard Majors and Janet Mancini Billson in *Cool Pose*, black women are assaulted and murdered "at a greater rate than do the intimate relationships of any other racial or ethnic group in the United States."[158] As vulnerable scapegoats, black women serve as unwilling surrogates upon whom black men can vent their seething rage without fear of reprisal, with impunity, as opposed to that threatening citadel of white patriarchy with its distorted definitions of manhood. The black woman, less ominous and debilitating than the vengeful, mob wrath of white manhood, suffers the cruel reprises of her black partner's wounded male pride, painfully visible in the battle scars of abuse, battering and death. The fact that race and poverty select black women for that high risk category of physical and intimate violence? Greater risk for intimate violence incurs if she and her partner are a cohabiting couple. The fact is, some black men, far too many, feel that, even if they can't exert control over how they are treated in society, they will control "their women." Their use of physical force against black women as means to defining manhood leaves in its twisted wake futile fragmentation and divisiveness in the black community, inevitably setting up the community to self-destruct from within. Lamentably, this is what's passed on to young male teens foraging in street culture, gang affiliation, and through mastering criminal activities for their manhood. Columnist and writer Ellis Cose warns black brothers, young and old, to weigh carefully the consequences of their actions before succumbing to blood-letting violent rage:

> Resisting the temptation to turn loved ones into targets can sometimes be extremely difficult, but before giving in to temptation, we should remind ourselves that those who love us are the best hope we have to regain whatever humanity we have lost; that they, in other words, are our salvation."[159]

Brothers have yet to learn that sisters are not the enemy. Unacceptable on any terms, black-on-black domestic violence must halt its unbridled wrath upon the ill-used bodies and difficult lives of black women.[160]

Boys II Men: The Crisis of Fathering and Mentoring

I'm practically grown. And you talkin' I need you. You crazy or somethin' Man? Do you know what my Momma went through? My Momma taught me how to ride a bike, tie a tie. She even told me how to use a condom so I wouldn't be some brother with an unwanted baby like you. You want to come back into the picture and tellin' me I need you.

Junior from Get on the Bus

Activist intellectual Haki R. Madhubuti talks bluntly about the present plight of black boys in black America in his book, *Claiming Earth*: "If anything is clear about the African-American community today, it is that Black women are having serious difficulty teaching Black boys to be men and, by extension, to be fathers."[161] Mudhubuti's counsel comes tested from the difficult trenches of his own embattled experience as a survivor of his own urban manchild's tale, an abandoned son reared by a drug-addicted, single mother. But unlike so many of our black male leaders and intellectuals, who still declare late Senator Daniel Patrick Moynihan correct when it comes to berating black mothers for failing to raise strong black sons, Madhubuti does not join that choir. As has been the case, since Moynihan's 1965 Report on "The Negro Family"[162] was first released, the blame for decades has been tossed upon this mysterious, mystical, so-called black matriarchal power for emasculating the identity of the black male. Less interested in such critical factors as race, class, gender, even socioeconomic forces in destabilizing as well as emasculating black manhood, scapegoating vulnerable black women had more political currency. Moynihan availed himself of the best political ploy in a belligerent sixties' racial context. He targeted black women as the black man's problem, rather than addressing adverse conditions constrained by historical and socially determined factors. Up to this day, stigmatizing black women for thwarting black men from achieving their destiny as the strong patriarchal leader "nature" intended them to be interferes precipitously into black male and female relationships.[163]

True to its divisive origins, "much" gone wrong with the black family continues to be dumped on the iconic shoulders of that mythic black "superwoman."[164] She, in essence, emerges in a racially biased and sexist history as the root source of a pervasive pathology embroiling the black family, and is so condemned as problematic to the "proper" social evolution of gender relations in the black community. In all of this, the role of society has never truly been fully interrogated in refusing equal access to all men, especially to its norms of manhood. "American society has not provided many black males with legitimate channels or resources for developing a strong sense of masculinity, status, and respect."[165] So Madhubuti's words, in contrast to much that has been bantered about in unsympathetic public forums like the *Charlie Rose Show*, act as no condemnation; nor do they preach a socially acceptable disparaging of the genuine, sincere efforts of black women to rear male children with the full anticipation of them becoming contributing adult citizens.

From Mudhubuti's own fatherly practice, he does admit that rearing children alone is a difficult task for anyone. Political economist Julianne Malveax is quick to affirm, "Sisters are doing it alone, but they rather not." Author bell hooks echoes the wisdom of Mudhubuti. In one of her recent books, *We Real Cool: Black Men and Masculinity*, hooks is emphatic: "Boys, especially, need adult men to be role models to teach them how to negotiate patriarchy in ways that are not soul damaging, to show them how to work around the system, and to create healthy alternative self-concepts."[166] In a patriarchal society, raising black boys takes on mammoth proportions. Sean "P-Diddy" Combs funds the Daddy's House Social Programs, and I congratulate Mr. Combs on being sensitively intuitive in perceiving just how desperately black children long to call somebody daddy or, in actuality, just want their daddies. Their anger and frustration toward their fathers' absences run as deep as the love they yearn to give and receive from them. Forgiveness will not come without a mighty struggle for that gross unparental act of abandonment.

Tragically, these present fatherless homes are so reminiscent of black families being intentionally ripped apart, split up, and fragmented to adapt profit margins to the brute plantation economy. "Jumpin' the broom" offered the closest a black man could ever dream of having a legal family. Treated as chattel property without a human identity, lacking legal standing as an agent of choice, reduced to nothing more than live stock for heavy labor and a strapping stud for replenishing human stock—refused the black man the right to administer his status as a responsible male adult. Up till today, black fathering is political. In the final analysis, black people must determine and interpret what masculinity means, and what it looks like for our community's survival.

However, with or without male parental role modeling, an important order of business is to instill in adolescent males early on that fathering a child is no rite of passage from boyhood into adulthood. Children are no badge of honor for declaring manhood status. In fact, they are the real losers in this irresponsible equation. Because their wounds are invisible, and they (children) powerless, not enough absentee fathers weigh the lifetime wounds inflicted upon innocent children. Caught-up in the vicious cycle, some young absentee fathers accuse the lack of fatherly role models in their own lives for their irresponsible behavior and use it as an excuse to abandon their most sacred trust or responsibility. It borders on license. "My father wasn't there, so I don't have to be there either," is how some of the young men in my social science class described the attitude on the street corner. Truly unfortunate, fathering unwanted children has evolved as a way of life for countless black men. At its worst, it has posed a fortuitous way that black males have affirmed their prowess as a man without following through a similar commitment to fulfilling the accompanying fathering and economically supportive roles. Their kind of sexual promiscuity has taken a high toll on the black community's resilience, producing unprecedented households of absentee fathers. Then, too, sexual promiscuity in a HIV/AID world is a dangerous pursuit, with alarming rates of transmission in our afflicted community. Black women are paying some of the highest casualties in the nation. Following in the footsteps of far too many of their elders, young black males are imitating this irresponsible behavior at reckless numbers in producing babies without expectation of acting as a provider or father. In all reality, how high can expectations be of teenagers? when they need parenting themselves. But this uncensored and unrebuked behavior creates even fewer economically stable families. Aside from the unfathomable social and economic cost, the weight of absentee fathers in the black community deals a crushing blow, from which few recover, to the spirit and morale of our young.

More importantly, the crisis of absentee fathers shows up in black youth going to prison to reassure peers that they're "tough enough to take it," might have special appeal for youth drawn to gangs, but counts as no rite of passage to manhood. Nor does it possess any coveted currency for the black community. Instead, it leads inevitably to that dead-end trail of social death and disposability. Once, to be known as an ex-offender in the black community evoked effacing shame, and carried its own harsh stigma. Now, the status is so widespread that it bestows a dubious badge of survival honor, boasted as a fraternal rite of passage. Shame has been domesticated into a crude fact of black life until, for our youth, it assumes the face value of natural and not prickly bothersome. One of my students complained that in her neighborhood a parolee's release was celebrated with a picnic. Her question was pointed, "What honor did he deserve?" Prison experience gains awkward acceptance as a "stepping stone" to manhood. Unfortunately, too many youth are looking up to those in prison.[167] Regardless of the false sense of elevated self-esteem that manchildren might derive from navigating the distresses of this prison "manhood" rite of passage, a black mother confesses her parental sense of failure over her son's misdeed.

> My son was part of a gang drive-by shooting last year and was sent to prison. I don't know, I thought I was a good parent. I mean, I didn't raise him to be like that, I tried to give him and the rest of the kids what they needed. But I had to work and I couldn't be everywhere at once. I don't know, I just don't know anymore.

On this score, black mothers are emphatic: "That's not how I raised him."

With over 60 percent of black children living in fatherless homes, black mothers have little choice about not carrying the entire parenting load single-handedly. Most are desperately in need of support from extended family, friends and mentors—ask any single mother.

But African American children are in trouble. Being the least protected in society makes them most vulnerable to sexual predators, gang activity, alcohol and drug abuse, teen pregnancy, and delinquency. Thus, first and foremost, given the precarious times that the black community is traversing, black masculinity needs to be understood in terms of responsibility to the black child, the black woman, the black family. And even as I resist painting all black men with the broad stroke of a single brush, for countless many are extraordinary fathers, faithful to their responsibility, far too many are also absent, up to 60 percent. Black men must step up to the plate and take their place alongside black women to secure the emotional and survival needs of black children.

Together, they must nurture an environment for black children to flourish unmolested by street danger or soul bile, to buffer them from the onslaught of racist miseducation, emotional demoralization, and finally, to offer tutelage in scaling its death-trapped land mines planted along their path or snake pits awaiting their headlong stumble. Who else will teach them? Difficult, yes, no promises of ease, but despite the difficulty, it should be our grandest aspiration as parents to give black children strong roots to accelerate their flight into life's possibilities, shoulders to climb upon to launch them into their competitive advantage. Our just being there counts considerably as one of those essential ingredients for their life success, especially in the lives of impressionable manchildren. Black parents must nurture children into living souls by our life example. No one is going to do it for us, but us.

However, for black men and women, taking ownership of our responsibility does not absolve the government of its responsibility in leaving no citizen behind, in this case, no child behind. In my best opinion, this is where the moral responsibility crusades fall short—although I hear Cosby's cry, who will protect the children? the next generation, the most vulnerable of us all. Yet, in their overzealous near-sightedness to call black men and women accountable to their duties and responsibilities, their myopic vision falls short of a government's social responsibility. (Politicians are being accused of using absentee dads in the black community for political fodder, just to assure conservatives that they have shared values. In this pandering to a specific constituency at the expense of fair representation, concerned black men have every right to cry foul. I also agree that black men have been demonized all too often to represent the worst impulses of this nation, unfairly.) These passionate crusaders failed to apply an equal critique to the negligent actions of our government in abandoning the welfare of the public good. Certainly, when it comes to young black males, this nation is unprepared to ensure that they are supported in their efforts to become strong men, or that "leave no child behind"[168] requires giving all children the best chances for success. This is not about asking "the man" for undeserved handouts. By rights, all citizens should expect the government to be impartial, responsible to all of its citizens, and to provide a social safety net for its neediest citizens, that being, its voiceless children.

Finally, of this I am certain though, the black community has never posted notice that the black male role is bankrupt. Black men, in organizations such as 100 Black Men, are quite vocal about the black community's desperate need for responsible black fathers, natural or surrogate, to help black women raise our sons into strong men. Big Brothers organizations, churches, and other community groups canvas the halls and offices of high and low profile institutions across the nation, committing positive role models to teach fatherless sons and nephews male responsibility and accountability. "More black males need to become primary and -secondary- school teachers to provide role models and mentor students along the way," advocates Dr. Reginald Wilson, scholar emeritus at the American Council on Education. The other alternative is far too injurious for manchildren—abandoning them to Hollywood's stereotypes of male mentoring or to homicidal street autobiographies—either way could be just as deadly.

CHAPTER 5

Terrorism in the Media
Stereotypes of Black Masculine Identity

The Assassination of the Black Male Image
Earl Ofari Hutchinson

The key concern was Black cultural integrity: how have the very public images of young Blacks in hip hop music and culture affected the larger Black community? Central to this discussion was the pervasive use of offensive epithets in rap lyrics…, all of which reinforce negative stereotypes about Blacks. What was the price of this remarkable breakthrough in the visibility of young Blacks in the mainstream culture? Had young rappers simply transferred images of young Black men as criminals from news reports to entertainment?
Bakari Kitwana, *The Hip Hop Generation*

With not enough positive images of young black males in the popular media, and even less are worthy of role modeling, the public image dilemma of black males witnesses to the persistent travail of black masculinity in America. In probing this social plight at a deeper level, it pleads for a closer scrutiny of media stereotypes, and how they wage forms of racial and sexual terrorism against black manhood.

How the young black male image is negatively treated in the media has rightly raised serious concerns in the black community. Too often, native sons are brazenly projected in media propaganda as the extreme of a "gangsta" or thug stereotype. Or often portrayed from the other extreme is a vaguely familiar femininity reset in a masculine physique. Either is construed as their genetic and socio-psychological fulfillment, with hypersexuality appearing as the media's happy median. This negligent stereotyping of black males is aired through the venue of the visual mass media—network television is what

⑥⑨

I'm referring to most often in this work—and fed into the psychosocial veins of black boys. This is done, at a time, when perhaps more than at any other time in black history, black boys are most vulnerable and in need of responsible male role modeling and guidance. With few fathers in the home to role model for them black manhood, young boys are having a difficult time discovering this on their own. At such a time, youth are exploring deep psychological questions like: how do I become a man? How do I prove myself? How must I behave? Television commercials, acting as infomercials without critical censors, slip into their young minds their-not-so subtle messages of media stereotyping.

Rap videos have done little better with their obvious thug-like praise of the night life. Their videos feed a culture that glamorizes pejorative images like pimps and drug dealers, as well as the misogynistic exploitation of black women's bodies. Black male rappers have borrowed liberally from some of the worst images in American culture of black people. And they are quickly cashing in on this profane, threatening, and hypersexual black body eroticizing. Thus, the messages that rap videos communicate compound the social plight of what young black manhood looks like in America. Reinforcing the initial premise, not enough images of positive black males are available to assist young black males in their rite of passage into young manhood.

Commercials and Rap Videos Matter

Of particular concern is how network commercials are programming black boy's gaze with an ambivalent masculinity. According to one commercial sponsor, it's easier "to be like your mother" for young black boys than to explore what it's takes to grow up as a black manchild in combat-torn communities in the twenty-first century. As cast in another popular commercial, a basketball star dresses like an elderly black lady, trailed by the gaze of black boys who are repeating, "She's the man." Or a similar commercial entices a little black boy to think, "If I were Cinderella!" In a recent Burger King commercial, an adolescent male wishes to become a ballerina. The fact is, each time I see such commercialized propaganda, I ask myself, what is the meaning of this? when there are so few black male role models for black boys. Is this ideological warfare? Commercial propaganda such as this, aimed solely at the black audience, preys upon the impressionable gaze of many fatherless sons.

Deborah Prothrow-Stith, professor at the Harvard School of Public Health, shares her conclusions: "All the research indicates that boys in father-absent homes have great difficulty with sex roles and what's called gender identification; that is, the establishment of a satisfying identity as a male if you are a male...."[169] Counsel from one of the best educational authorities, Jawanza Kunjufu in *Countering the Conspiracy to Destroy Black Boys,* advises:

> It takes a man to develop boys into men.... I did not say a single female parent could not develop her son into a man, but ...until African American women admit that only men can make boys into men, and African American men become responsible for giving direction to at least one male child, the conspiracy will continue."[170]

One manchild channeled his anxieties into these rap lyrics, "I'm startin' to get worried without a pops I'll grow to be her." With the absences of so many black men from black homes and communities, who will teach the young males how to be men? Who would disagree? Black men need to be involved in the lives of black youth. But by now, all can concede that the television needs to stop mentoring black male children.[171] It will never provide the positive role model black boys sorely deserve.

To counter stereotyped images of this bold black male emasculation, rap artists in their controversial videos are filling in the void, but to the other dangerous extreme. They are expressing some of their own hidden angst about black manhood. This is not so in every case. Positive rappers like Public Enemy, Rakim, Kanye West, Kirk Franklin and other fine artists are producing positive messages with true-to-life images, and not the usual disparaged gangsta violence and misogyny. The problem is, many more rap videos push black masculinity to a detrimental edge with it being made symbolic with violence, thuggerism, and the vile exploitation of women. No matter how perverse, and unfortunately so, far too many young black male rappers have figured out that the straightest path to some semblance of masculinity in a white patriarchal society is through their identification as strong, conquering patriarchs. They adopt with facility the white patriarchal attitude over and against the feminized oppressed, such as black people, young black males, women and others. "Listen you've got to put that b— in her place, even if it's slapping her in her face" is a line in Snoop Dogg's "Can U Control Yo Hoe," for instance. It is suggestive of social victim turned into victimizer to escape the exploitation and marginalization associated with his socially subordinate status. Likewise, the homophobic biases found in rap lyrics are as much about the prejudices of gay bashing as they are about establishing this strong, virile image of the masculine withheld. Through the vehicle/voice that black rappers possess in shaping public opinion, young black males seek to be recognized as "somebody," not the docile feminized but the powerful masculine. However, this neither solves the riddle of black masculinity in white patriarchal society, nor does it place before young boys the positive role models parents badly yearn that they emulate. Yet, the masculine polarities that the black community contends with cannot persist by our own hands if we are expected to raise up a generation to survive the captivity of black masculinity in America.

Hollywood in Drag

To take my critique to another level, in an *Essence* column, actor Isaiah Washington voices a critical assessment of the restricted roles available to black males in the Hollywood studios of the television and film industry. He questions Hollywood's narrow depiction of African American male characters, which only churns out more uncensored stereotypes.

> This means I am no longer typecast only as the subhuman rapist, mugger or drug dealer; I can now also be the angst-filled drag queen.... It doesn't take a genius to conclude that the larger society finds a Black man in drag more credible than, say, the same man in an astronaut's space suit. I concede that some of our portrayals are unforgettable: Remember Flip Wilson's Geraldine? He helped many of us laugh away our homophobia. Then there was the Antonio Fargas character in Car Wash, Jamie Foxx's Wanda, Martin Lawrence's Sheneneh and now, of course, Ru Paul. When I look at these very talented and funny men, I can't help laughing. Yet I wonder if I should be crying instead, because these seem to be the only kind of Black men society finds acceptable.[172]

Look at the phenomenal success of Tyler Perry's Medea and Martin Lawrence dressed up as Big Momma. Those playing such ideological commercialized roles are no black-faced vaudeville puppets but the real McCoy. By giving us this media drag version of black male masculinity with black assent, ideological warfare trumps the question for a community at-risk to engage the question of what is black masculinity. What does it mean, how does it look, and how can it contribute to survival strategies? Those playing such ideological commercialized roles are no black-faced vaudeville puppets, but the real McCoy. Quite a switch, when during the height of the Civil Rights Movement, black men were fairly united in their insistence that they must have their manhood, like *any white man*. Rallying for black males to adopt characteristics of a socially construed femininity is just as problematic as requiring a socially imposed masculinity, when gender itself is shifting through a battlefield of fierce social and cultural contestations. In some social circles, the expected meaning and performance of a given gender refuse to be taken for granted. Again, I ask, what are the implications of this for a community at-risk? when we live in a society that does not obey the biblical injunction: "neither male nor female." We live in a well-defined patriarchal dispensation which polices all acts of gender difference, pathologizes them, and paints much of them with a black face to which the conservative right genuflects in unthinking assent.

The Art of Media Domination

A typical dose of black males as boys, irresponsible, immature, hypersexual or "doggish" greets us on the silver screen on too many occasions to be dismissed as child's play. Recently McDonald's released a Black History Month commercial exploiting the supposedly "dog" nature of black males, nicely tempoed to the dangerous innocence of its jingle, "lovin it."[173] Media stereotypes, whether in the film industry or routine commercials, build upon either manipulating a projected hyper-sexuality or effeminate constitution of black males. Such compromising messages about captive black manhood are prepackaged for media marketing and exported around the world where they are consumed as holy writ. As the contested images gain global appeal, they become the distorted lens through which the world sees and seeks black masculinity. At home, the film industry does little better. The "sexual-ploitation" stereotypes weary me to the point that I shy away from going to the movies nowaday. I am afraid of witnessing these nether images ridiculing black male striving for any kind of righteous masculinity. From all likely accounts, the media is not invested in the empowering of the black male image. To do so is to jeopardize its own community's sense of self or survival that has evolved based upon the dehumanization of black humanity, black manhood.

Subsequently, I simply err on the side that the media is conscious of its image-making power. Certainly, media factories like Hollywood and other sectors of the entertainment and communication industry wield enormous power over manufacturing consent about what is acceptable social perception.[174] To what extent? Consider the millions of dollars that are budgeted for the launching of a new product campaign or introducing a presidential candidacy. Just these few examples argue the primary role of the media in shaping public opinion. The empire power that the media possesses in masterminding public consent is not lost on network powerbrokers and politicians. "From the global resources of the ABC network," brags its nightly news presentation to viewers. Thus, the media's not-so-innocent danger to at-risk communities is what this essay is assessing in part. "The values disseminated by transnational media enterprises secure not only the undisputed cultural hegemony of popular culture, but also lead to the depoliticization of social relation and the weakening of civic bond."[175] In other words, the media's power runs deep, gifted with the unfettered ability to run roughshod over any community's resistance to stereotypes. It can conspire to disrupt the process of society or buttress the elitist arrogance of powerbrokers. It all depends upon who's doing the buying. Absolute power surely corrupts absolutely. Be assured, with the media asking meaningless questions like "Is Britney Spears pregnant?" It will not save us.

To gain a better sense of media domination in the public square, consider how quickly the concentration of media power fell into the hands of a few corporations. It was a 2003 coup led by former chairman Michael Powell on behalf of wealthy corporations, with their well-heeled lobbyists. From the bloody skirmish, a handful of corporations prevailed as the primarily beneficiaries, not the American people. Nor was the victorious emergence of this new monopoly power lost on the protestors of this sinister consolidation of important free speech venues in America. Now the American public finds itself genuflecting before nightly news' infomercials as a routine substitute for real news about the world. Sadly, news has degenerated to sports's highs and lows, the weather, crime and entertainment; there is very little Peabody Awards quality journalism.

Just how much of a behemoth the broadcast media is, is confirmed by its ability to streamline news on any given day. Although different stations are supposedly independent networks on the surface, but with the amassing of network power into the hands of the few, the public is force-fed the same point of view; the same news program line-up prevails. No matter how much one switches the channel for a different feature, always with more commercials than news, but the same stories on NBC, CBS, ABC, Fox News ensue. As any frustrated consumer, the customer must satisfy himself or herself with the scarce menu of the day of what corporate culture ordains as "bottom-line" newsworthy.

Finally, what does it mean when news is a pretext for advertisement or entertainment? News as advertisement could not have been more obvious than when, under the cover of newsworthy, Fox's CW 9 and 11 informed the "loyal" public of Don Imus' return to the radio waves. What a clever idea to use the news anchors and their so-called legitimacy to inform America that a fallen star returns to the radio airwaves, washed clean, and restored to grace by his earning potential for New York's WFAN-AM! The same goes for hip hop DJ Star's return to Power 105 after allegedly uttering threats of a sexual nature against a colleague DJ's daughter. Star's carefully orchestrated return coincided "providentially" with Imus' to disperse public dissent of anything racial or discriminatory at work. Supposedly, the message to the public is that they are both damaged goods, and there's nothing racial about it either. (I err on the side that two wrongs don't make a right.) Skeptically, I wonder whether all this was really newsworthy or another attempt to use "news" to promote and legitimate Imus' return to diminish the repulsion that his personality, and even the very mention of his name, evokes for black women.

As in the case of black males, there is a media manufacturing of consent about their thug nature, hyper-sexuality, or effeminate nature for purposes other than service to the black community. Seemingly, the black community is doing too little to dispute the dissemination of such injurious propaganda about black manhood.[176] But how the American media emasculates the identity of black boys and men achieves no harmless effect. These young boys, especially, are drawn into an uninitiated soul conflict about their identity within the context of rampant, white male aggression, domination, and supremacy—reinforcing an already unequal balance of power that white society seeks to maintain at all costs, unquestioned. What I am arguing is that some psycho-social anxiety played out in the lives of manchildren does not belong to them, but is sparked by other survival interest, this besieging of them from within their own soul.

At the same time, the moral caution incumbent upon the black community is not to demonize those of a different sexual orientation. But this is a clarion call to act, protect, and guide all manchildren into fulfillment and self-actualization.

"Chappelle in a Dress": Terrorism at Home and Abroad

In an *Oprah* interview, Dave Chappelle, one of the star comedians of *Comedy Central*, who left the show abruptly in 2005 during his third season, said the final straw for him was when the writers wrote a skit with him in a dress.[177] He queries, "Why is it that white people always want to put us in a dress?" No paranoia here, Dave is on to something. In most patriarchal cultures, the height of insult to injury is to emasculate a man's dignity and sense of masculinity in any way, either by word or deed. Chapelle's protest is of no innocent matter, and helps to make my point more apparent about the sexual terrorism practiced upon black male identity. In particular, judge President Bush's behavior after the September 11 attack (9/11) in U.S. foreign policy. His obsession in bringing Osama Bin Laden to vigilante justice, "dead or alive," paraded upon the world stage was to simulate a strong, virile masculinity and not a whimpered 9/11 victimhood. Bush, the voice of America's male pride, refused to be held hostage to a terrorist image of national defeat. His gauntlet-sounding words boasted a wild-west swagger, reminiscent in the American mind of that iconic John Wayne's manliness; a throwback to the days of cowboy, pistol-whipping lawlessness is indeed not the traditional reserved statesman's diplomacy. To this point, some of that rugged combat aggression playing out in Iraq today is really about the injury to, as well as redemption of, the white masculine identity in America, "patriotism" aside; although the war effort had been religiously evangelized as bringing modern democracy to the "backward" or "uncivilized" parts of the Muslim world. If the bold truth be told, the surprise attack of 9/11 was experienced as an injury not-to-be-borne by the proverbial phallocentric, white male macho power committed by those whom western powerbrokers deemed as expendable and non-threatening—people of color of a suspicious religious persuasion. In their revenge-driven ardor for payback justice, the U.S. world powerbrokers, alias World Trade Organization (WTO), spewed out hostility as foreign policy diplomacy, namely through its anointed representative, President Bush, Jr. (Read as: the Muslim enemy combatants must pay for this perception of injury to white male power and authority.)

In the case of Iraq, caught in the quagmire of this global imbalance of power, it presented itself tactically as an attractive proposition to stake a U.S. "savior" presence to deal with those "terrorist infidels," supposedly holding "hostage" the oil fields of the Middle East from capitalist intrusion. Such missionary propaganda rebukes any truth-telling history, sure to condemn America as global invaders. To legitimize the invasion, Sadam

Hussein was caricatured as the Stalin of the Middle East, whereas it became incumbent upon, if not the necessary "sacrificial duty" of, the U.S. government to oust this grotesque dictator. But regardless of how elaborate the U.S.'s political mystification, the bloodsucking thirst of the WTO for empire did not dupe the world community, and remains offensive to this day.[11] In this scenario, the benevolent missionaries of "democratic mercy," the U.S. soldiers, that is, gained "legal" access for multinational corporations to plunder unmercilessly oil reserves as wartime spoils or exact Abu Ghraib penance for uncorroborated terrorist sins of 9/11. In any case, neither Osama bin Laden nor weapons of mass destruction were ever recovered. But clearly, here were all the trappings of a twenty-first century-style crusade being waged on behalf of global capitalism or its concocted version of an old-style inquisition to rid the world of uncapitalist "infidels", who are antagonistic to a western empire-building hegemony. Insurgent is their other name. (The final message was: let the war in Iraq send a clear message to all potential Al-Qaeda operatives, enemy combatants, and hostile insurgents who refuse a western global empire-hunt in order to consolidate world domination, that their arrogant insolence will not be tolerated by an empire-wielding nuke-ready arsenal.)

What this all means—with no discernable weapons of mass destruction ever surfacing in Iraq, unless the person of Saddam Hussein now falls into that dubious category, but in truth because there never were any—as articulated by its most visible spokesman, the President Bush, is that white American males were taken by incredulous surprise wrapped as they were in their own god-cocoon of white male economic imperialism. Challenging their time-honored definition of masculinity was what the terrorist attack accomplished also. Fermented in the wake of 9/11 was a feeling of impotence experienced by white males about their inability to protect their land, their material wealth, certainly their property and possessions—be it in the guise of women, children, or economic domination—their formula for manhood. And from that revenge-driven rage, *homeland* security was born.

But here forms the critical link about sexual terrorism practiced upon the black male identity. Efforts at conquering and subduing enemy combatants, as were seen at Abu Ghraib Prison, required dehumanizing and sexually emasculating male prisoners as part of the interrogation program. As political psychiatrist Frantz Fanon rightly assesses, "We know how much of sexuality there is in all cruelties, tortures, beatings."[179] Modified tactics of emasculation prevail, of course, for black male civilians in the U.S., but that does not preclude their insidious intent at unconditional subordination. Primarily, U.S. emasculating tactics against black males are manipulated through official transcriptions like the controversial Moynihan Report, media sitcoms, movie entertainment, commercials, the restricted roles for black male actors, police raids on them that often leave one too many sodomized, and that every unprovoked "justified homicide." The end result proves detrimental in breaking the human spirit as well as crippling the will of those identified as "predators," infidels, or enemy combatants, or the "Negro Problem," whether domestic black Americans or internationals occupying combat arenas like Iraq.

In my final word on this, can the black community casually dismiss psychiatrist Frances Cress Welsing's words? "White males fully understand that males who are forced to identify as [passive] will be programmed simultaneously into submission to the male they call 'The man,' as opposed to aggression against those same men."[180] As such, is it an ostensible conspiracy to emasculate our sons' social testosterone and displace any image that displays socially acceptable "boys will be boys" impulses with a benign male clone? How does the idea of the "only kind of Black man society finds acceptable" functions in diminishing for the manchild any heroic image of the black male as protector of his family and property, with the right to exist unharassed? when he is ever cast as the helpless prey of slave masters and lynch mobs, of Night Riders and the

Ku Klux Klan, of police brutality and of intracommunal violence. As Dr. Adelaide L. Sanford, Vice Chancellor of the Board of Regents of the State of New York, is quoted as saying at a National Urban League panel:

> The education system most visible in this country is not an education of liberation, but one of dependence. If they talk about chattel slavery, they don't teach about the insurrections and the measures enslaved people took to get their freedom. What African-American teenager wants to identify [himself] with a person who was born a slave and died a slave?[181]

What noble instances of black male pride like "Black Power" or "We Shall Overcome" revolutionary resistance are being subtly recast in the media as symbolizing gang violence or the latter as handkerchief-head Negroes—better known as Uncle Tom weaklings—to dispute black males claiming their radical identity as strategic, most times non-violent, political insurrectionists against unjust state violence and injustices?[182] With black manchildren having so few heroes to feed their moral imagination of black manhood fighting for social justice and defending human rights, does this demoralization by the media and social powerbrokers presumably eliminate the visible threat of another bereted community of fearless Black Panthers? Because the assumption is that, when the image of the strong man is broken, then the community of "women" will submit. One mandate is irrefutably clear: to develop and affirm our own community's concept of black masculinity. Acknowledged from the outset, there could very well be shared elements with white masculine identity, but its point of departure evolves from what advantages the black community's survival, and not another's.

In all of this, as the disruptive narrative of civil rights protest came marching into America's historical consciousness to agitate for change in race relations in this country, with all of its unruly political messiness, the burden of remembering that past is equally ours to empower another generation. Why? Because at every level from the stereotypical or the ideological, to the threat of peoplehood extinction, clearly we are a community in struggle. Thus, black people must tell our freedom story of pre-and-post civil rights history any way we can in order to prevent our unedited version being lost to the selective memory of the powers-that-be or pimped by Hollywood's revisionist storytellers. Else, it will be revised to the point that everybody saved black folks but our own humble hands.[183] Such proposes an empowering legacy of hope to leave to vulnerable black manchildren!

CHAPTER 6

"A Crisis On Our Hand"
Black-on-Black Teen Violence

I pledge that from this day forward I will strive to love my brother as I love myself.

From the Pledge of the Million Man March

Whatever happened to apologies like "I'm sorry," "excuse me," or if you want to be hip about it, "my bad"?

One teen inquires

Although the Justice Department boasts of crime being down, young black male homicides show little sign of letting-up in certain inner-city communities. An angry storm of teen violence yet surges throughout urban streets, for even the most trivial of matters, leaving a flood of juvenile carnage in its onerous wake. From across the nation, peppering the evening news is the chronic homicidal reports of young black males as killers or killed. In Norfolk, Virginia, a black seventeen-year-old male shot and killed another young black man, allegedly over a girl. High school student Chris Garner escaped his tough Memphis, Tennessee neighborhood, away from the fighting, the crime, and the murder of a friend as he stood alongside, splattered with the taste of fresh blood. Grudges, debts, drug deals gone awry, gang vengeance are all sorted out with a gunshot blast. In the 14-17 years old age group, black males are six times as likely to be a homicide victim.

Being black and male in America, as an understated fact of his existence, is to live life at-risk. The jeopardy increases exponentially if he is a young teen male. In record numbers, as high as 90 percent, the victims of young black male killers are other young black men. They have the highest firearm homicide rate of any demographic group.[184] What these deadly statistics poll is that an estimated one out of every 21 black American males will be murdered in his lifetime, most at the hands of another black male. From all accounts, research confirms that at the greatest risk are young black males walking this nation's city streets. A relatively recent study corroborates the "endangered" status of young teen males. A 2000 Report compiled by the ultraconservative Heritage Foundation on "Young African American Males: Continuing Victims of High Homicide Rates in Urban Communities"[185] cites that a 15-year old, urban, African American male faces an average probability of one in 45 that he will be a victim of homicide before reaching his 45th birthday.[186] His 15-year old white counterpart has a low one-in-185 probability of being a victim of homicide before his 45th birthday. For Washington, D.C., still considered the murder capital of American cities, a black male 15-year old stands a one-in-12 chance of being murdered before his 45th birthday.[187] In the 14-24 age group, manchildren account for 17 percent of the victims of homicide, and are 30 percent of the offenders, compared to their white counterparts who comprise 10 percent of the homicides and 17 percent of the perpetrators. Manchildren in urban areas are most at-risk to be murderers or murdered. Black youth die the fastest and in record numbers.

"A Second Paycheck"

Calculate poverty into the risk equation, and the numbers climb to epidemic proportions. Poverty cuts across the combination of social factors to outdistance even race in judging the manchild's vulnerability to homicide. Social scientist Andrew Hacker, in his *Two Nations: Black and White, Separate, Hostile, Unequal,* does not reduce manchildren's life chances to the injurious role of poverty alone. His analysis supports the complex interplay of intrusive social conditions into the lives of manchildren to explain the catastrophic violence menacing them. Even though he argues against singling out any one social factor as the catchall, with that said, Hacker also recommends "a second paycheck" in those impoverished single-parent homes. The benefit of the second paycheck is analogous to homes with both biological parents. In other words, according to the Juvenile Offenders and Victims 2006 National Report, juveniles "had lower lifetime prevalence of law-violating behaviors than did juveniles who lived in single parent families."[188] Committed to the redemption of the black male image in his vastly popular book, *The Assassination of the Black Male Image*, author Earl Hutchinson fingers poverty in more decisive terms than Hacker.

> There was never any hard evidence that boys raised in one-parent families were being groomed as high school drop-outs, drive-by shooters, dope dealers, and gang-bangers. If some were, it was not because of absentee father but because of absentee income."[189]

Hutchinson takes the side that if this nation were united and equal, race alone could not decide a victim's susceptibility to homicidal execution. Economic status would figure more prominently as the assassin. With the collusion of race and poverty to seal the manchild's death fate, he ends up as the nation's most vulnerable to homicide.

The fact is, with significant numbers of manchildren poor from their black birth, already they are estranged from that other America by the social divide that indulges in the pejorative meanings attached to icons peculiar to black urban life—the projects, public housing, inner-city, urban sprawl—where many black children live and wage war to grow up. Chronic conditions, tied to a spade of hostile social, educational, family, and economic circumstances, trump black youth's hard-earned lives. In many cases, the homes where they grow up qualify for TANF[12] support or other government subsidized services, usually headed by single females.[13] Children are trapped in that social phenomenon called the feminization of poverty. According to a national average, at least half of imprisoned youth's families are headed by single mothers, whose annual household income falls below the poverty level. Within those homes, few to none of the youth can claim role models who hold jobs within mainstream society or who supposedly practice values that do not rely upon a knife or a gun. Among these youth, violence is often witnessed as an inevitable fact of everyday life. "From my earliest recollections," a manchild sketches a picture of pervasive violence as ever-present to his environment, and was as natural as the air he breathed, "there has been struggle, strife, and the ubiquity of violence. This ranged from the economic destitution of my family to the domestic violence between my parents, from the raging gang wars to the omnipresent occupational police force in hot pursuit."[193] In an everyday, violence-infested context, black youth find that it prevails as an appalling fact of just how to stay alive, living constantly on the very precipice of disaster. Accordingly, what does that say about this generation of youth poised to take over the black community's destiny? Are they ready? vulnerable as they are to risk factors like failure in school, gang violence and inadequate guidance for their troubled lives.

Back to the Future: An Endangered Species

In her co-authored work, *Deadly Consequences: How Violence Is Destroying Our Teenage Population,* medical professional Deborah Prothrow-Stith backs up her claim of a brewing public health crisis in the black community regarding the violent at-risk status of young black males, with hard-hitting statistical data and compelling critical analyses. In the early nineties, she was arguing forcefully how deadly destructive and life crippling the scourge of violence was to jeopardizing manchildren's surviving; and the difficulty they face of being left unharmed and unmolested by belligerent social conditions. This brief excerpt from Prothrow-Stith's book gives some perspective on her dire warning to the national public health community. It also clarifies the race and class of those susceptible to violent attack, which also hand-picks the gender most likely to suffer from violent reprisals:

> Class and race often determine who will die. Most homicide victims are poor. Half the victims are ...black, although blacks comprise only 12 percent of the population. Of the young victims 15 to 24, blacks outnumber whites by four to one. Black males faced the greatest risk...."[194]

Before the publishing of Prothrow-Stith's book, research set forth in the late eighties by sociologist Jewelle Taylor Gibbs in her edited book, *Young, Black, and Male in America: An Endangered Species*, tracked this growing downward trend. Gibbs used the term "the new morbidity" to describe how young black males were overrepresented in deaths caused by homicide, accident, and suicide. Drug and alcohol abuse, according to her, played a major role in most of these deaths. Combined, they accounted for over 75 percent of deaths among young black men between 15-24 years old. Her groundbreaking work finds a striking parallel in corroborating death and incarceration statistics of today. For the black community and public health policy-makers, their research conveyed early on that without comprehensive social intervention to stem this fierce tide of unchecked aggression, young black males are truly bordering on the verge of becoming an "endangered species."

Not just a past epidemic, bearing witness to this horrific truth, death memoirs diarying this record demise in black America today are overflowing. An emotionally distraught mother, Hazel Rankin, longs for the day when black youth in America will stop killing each other. "I wish they would just stop," she confesses.[195] "We've lost so many friends," mourned Ashley Campbell, a friend of the slain Blair Holt. "You just feel so helpless."[196] As one mother whose son was recklessly killed charges, "There is a war on black men, one waged externally—an objective analysis of the statistics concerning who goes to jail for certain crimes and who doesn't reveals that." Just as importantly, she also recognizes that there is the internal war black men wage against each other as well. Her angst-riddled question, "How do you fight on two fronts?" lacks any definitive answer. For the latter, some mothers react by opting to send their children to the safety of boarding schools, outside of harm's way. During the lawless reign of segregation, sending children away was a survival tactic quite intimate to the black community. Black mothers wanted to spare their children the indignities of a separate and unequal world as well as a second-class education. But how many white mothers have had to send their children away to safety, fearing street retribution? Separation from our children returns the black community to auction block politics.

Ironically, many fled North to escape the over-zealous threat of a lynch mob death. However, the lynch mob is not the problem these days. "These kids know their immediate predator isn't the amorphous white system chipping away at their civil liberties, it's the little knucklehead next door with the semiautomatic."[197] As for those children who cannot leave battle zones, most accept that fearing for their lives is an urban rite of passage. This fear grown native to the rite of passage of black youth is less of the Emmitt Till's unrighteous mob version but gangs' turf obstacle courses where children must safely navigate minefields to make it successfully to school and back home alive. Though not unusual, in an attempt to circumvent violent, deathly encounters, many children take the long road home or alternate their routes to secure their lives. Clementina Chéry of Dorchester, MA, mother of slain teen Louis Brown, "changed Louis's bus stop to keep him safer."[198] After all her trying, she still could not save him. Lisa Oliver of East Baltimore takes her younger son, 14-year old Stephen, to school or waits for him at the bus stop after the murder of her older son, 16-year old James Lynch. Though Stephen complains of being upset at friends teasing him as a "momma's boy," Lisa prefers his humiliation to ID-ing another son on a slab at the county morgue.[199]

Primary victims of black male criminals are other black males. Resolving trivial conflicts by shooting one another to death is too often common. "In the black world they kill for gym shoes or leather jackets," worse still, for some "dimly perceived notion of respect."[201] Yes, in the manchild's do-or-die bid for that elusive honor, "respect," it signifies a deadly hunt among black youth as they tackle identity struggles. Sooner than address their feelings of low self-esteem and the absence of public faith in their "somebodiness," street aggression has become equated with a mistaken notion that "respect" is clawed from the mouth of an enemy prey, rather than earned between equals. "Too many of our young black males believe that manhood is defined by the ability to injure or damage another man." At a latent level, their fixation upon acquiring that forbidden fruit, "respect," sounds like a wounded cry for human recognition in a society which withholds its acceptance at every turn by insisting upon their human invisibility, gangster visibility, but indeed their overall powerlessness. Their "madd" indiscriminate search for power terminates in a true loss of power, invariably forfeited in their being invariably apprehended by policing authority, incarcerated, or their premature death. Yet, "to understand how Black manhood functions in the ghetto is to know, positively, that respect is the only currency that matters, the true taste of power. Without respect you have nothing and are regarded as less than nothing."[202]

A Crisis on Our Hand

We have a crisis on our hands. And although a black male death will most surely be at the hands of another black male, the fears of black mothers are no less abiding. Class position favors some sons with a limited number of viable options. But choosing life or death for a child is no less daunting for any mother. For many poorer sisters, women with fewer choices living in high-risk neighborhoods, the lack of choice is tantamount to a death sentence for their child.

With few buffer zones to secure their manchild's survival, many black mothers are fighting alone in the trenches this senseless death. Hear one mother's lost plea, crying out hopelessly for help, as she calls into the local radio station 1400AM seeking the community's 911 assistance in protecting, or better stated, "saving" her son:

Her call was frantic, and whose wouldn't be? faced with the unthinkable execution of her child, because he simply exists as black, young, and male, and she helpless to prevent it. A neighborhood bully, another teen, no more than 14, is terrorizing her son with a reckless handgun— hunting for his life. Her son solicits her help, begging   for his life, for her protection or he would have to be "packing something" to protect himself; and that might mean another black fratricide. An innocent son of even fewer choices, he was, if any at all, except shoot back. *Children, they are, who want to cry, to sob painfully over the lost spoils of their lives before they have had a chance to live, but they dare not for being thought as weak and a chump—in two words, not cool.*

No apparent reason could be discerned why her teen son was being menaced, other than that her boy was alive, black, male and at that vulnerable age where he was perceived as threatening and yet meaningless, all at the same time. Triple jeopardy—young, black, and male—sentenced him to premature death. In the eyes of his antagonist, the racist inscription carved upon his own lost life was displaced to another black male. Complaining to the police department gained little support because, according to "the book," a crime had not been committed. Running out of options, she was. To this single, black mother's aching pleas for help intervention, the sympathetic host sent out a community S.O.S. on the radio waves to the listening audience. In the end, this black mother may have felt desperately alone. And perhaps, she was.

"Now I just have to make it through the summer without getting shot," a teenage son solemnly advises his Mom while preparing to leave that fall for boarding school. These deathly worries multiply the youthful trials of black children, still. And although there was a large decline in the homicides committed by juveniles from the mid-1990s to 2002, in urban communities, young black males continue to show high homicide incidences.[203] How many white mothers have had to send their children away to safety, fearing street retribution? Separation from our children returns the black community to auction block polities. I often think, as opposed to securing the crime scene after an act of violence, the priority needs to shift. Put a yellow ribbon around the boundaries of our breathing children and demand that the hostile public not cross the limits of their bodily integrity.

This focus upon the fears of black mothers, moreover, does in no way tokenize the aching anxieties of black fathers.

CHAPTER 7

State Property: Black Prisoners

I wish people would stop viewing black males as dangerous, thinking we're all killers and rapists. I don't have any answers to the problems of crime. All I can do is keep going to school and lead by example.

Chris Garner, a high school student

The impulse to imprison black men now stretches to include the man-child. Frightened by a few highly publicized juvenile crimes, politicians began imposing harsher sanctions on juvenile offenders in the early 1990s. Predictably, the lash has fallen more frequently on black and brown boys than white.

The Washington Post

When a vision of unholy violence flashes through a white mind, rarely is a thought given to the billy club plunger sodomizing a defenseless Abner Louima or that bloodbath oozing from unlawful wounds of an unarmed man, murdered with 40 shots or so—all neatly done at the sinister hand of police brutality; but a black youth holding a furious looking handgun is made the culprit. Not nightmares of the NYPD's vigilante thirst for black male bloodsport—Sean Bell, only the most recent victim—Rodney King's violent LAPD gang-style beatdown, Emmett Till's mob execution, the unhooded crusaders of Howard Beach, New Jersey Turnpike's racial profilers, the blue and gray on paramilitary patrols, only black adolescent boys are summoned to mind as society's dark "predators." Not ghettoized education, staggering imprisonment, Iraq-type global war, drug war casualties, urban decay and poverty, systemic racial exclusion, nor all the other subtle and insidious forms of uncensored violence natural to discriminated life, in the lottery of choice black youth are surrendered as scapegoats for the sake of the greater social violence perpetrated against and upon them. From a 2001 study- in Allegheny County, Pennsylvania, "...Black youths were more likely to be charged as adults, more likely to be wrongly charged, more likely to be denied transfers to juvenile court and more likely to be sentenced to longer terms."[205]

"We Got to Punish Them"

Entrapped in an institutional web of racial bias and violence signals that black boys live life on probationary time. With their arrest already anticipated, rarely are their misdeeds casually regarded under the privileged prerogative of boyish pranks, "it's just a phase," or chalked up to "boys will be boys," or charitably excused with "the boy made a stupid mistake." For the slightest misdemeanor, the judicial system wastes no time in exercising the strong arm of the law, posed for a game plan of "three strikes, you're out" or mandatory sentencing.[206] Although young people in this country, typically if they are white, are traditionally viewed as childlike and "meriting guidance," black youth, on the other hand, have no such luck. They are refused any such benevolent coddling by the juvenile justice system, which habitually transfer them on for adult prosecution. On the one hand, a 12-year old may be offered up as either a fully responsible young adult to stand trial or a lawless predator, on the other. Either way, manchildren are condemned to incarceration in juvenile prisons or placed among adult populations for punishment in reckless numbers.

The pervasiveness of this racial myopia afflicts our manchildren with a tyrannical double standard, where they are always disparaged as social menaces and super-predators, just because "they be"—simply because they exist. Even before they are ever handcuffed for a crime, when law enforcement officials think black youth, they think drugs and "We've got to punish them." Yes, their fragile agency is battered daily with an unfair suspicion of wrongdoing. When advocating for black youth as redeemable and rehabilitatable, such an unpopular position is persistently rebuked by the public outcry of "going soft on crime." But what is not accounted for is that the public fixation on projecting black youth as the nation's worst nightmare misses the cries of the Columbines waiting to happen. America must stop devouring her young and reach out with care to all of them, in the hope of saving as many as she can—black, Asian, Latino, and white.

But let them commit a crime. Young black males are so quickly vilified with the thug label in the public forum that innocent until proven guilty resounds as the hypocritical rhetoric it truly is in their lives. In contrast, for similar crimes, their white counterparts are regarded as "misguided" youth and gang "wannabes," never assumed endowed with inherently criminal tendencies of a predatory nature.

One of the more visible tragedies happening in the black community is the number of black male teens and men being rounded up in the criminal justice system on any given day. The black community has yet to calculate fully the human losses incurred from this mass exodus, instigated by incarceration. But, indeed, this exportation into judiciary lockdown is of such magnitude that it's now possible to visit black neighborhoods where most of the young men have disappeared, where families spend their Sundays visiting their incarcerated loved ones...."[207] The following statistics highlight how out-of-hand the numbers have escalated: one out of every three young black males is imprisoned, on parole or under the policing authority of the US law enforcement. In Baltimore, Maryland, half of all African-American men in their 20s find themselves either incarcerated or under criminal justice system supervision. "You've got one in five young black men living in a cage.... I saw that 'one in five' figure for Baltimore, and I wanted to cry."[208] It's common knowledge that a young black male could more easily be on lockdown than attending college.

Mass Incarceration as National Policy

The social and economic capital each male member potentially forfeits to the new prison plantations has not been tallied in its human losses to black survival and progress. In other words, human investments that the black community stands sorely in need of are daily appropriated for the expansion of the prison industrial complex, on the rise as a major U.S. growth industry. What has not been clearly calculated by the black community is how the incarceration of our young black sons figures prominently into the sinister scheme of prison expansion and escalation. And until we do, this mass incarceration practiced as national policy will continue, only increasing in its sinister targeting of young black life. An advocate for black males, journalist Earl Ofari Hutchinson's pessimism is well-founded, "The entrenchment of racially biased drug laws, racial profiling, and chronic poverty in many black communities means that more black men will be arrested, prosecuted, convicted and serve longer prison sentences than white men."[209]

As of 2001, almost 17 percent of all black men, nearly two million in total, had some prison experience. Now, one in three endures some form of supervision in the justice system; as projected for 2020, it will be two out of every three black males.[210] In certain cities, one in four of all black males languishes in prison, on probation, or is on parole. Compared to over a decade ago, one of every ten black males was reported as having had experience with the criminal justice system.[211] How are we to explain such a high incarceration rate in the black community? Are blacks just more prone to commit crimes, a blind casualty of natural selection that leads to jail or prison? I cautiously ask. Or does this high incarceration rate result from complicit social factors that have little to do with nature? Research isolates a critical factor that aids in explaining the disproportionate number of sentences in the black community: the nation's war on drugs.

In actual fact, the war on drugs was fought out in distressed black neighborhoods, on low-level dealers, targeted because white suburbia posed a more formidable field of attack with its legal and economic fortresses. Few question the close correlation between the "war on drugs," gang activity, and the growth of the prison industrial complex. The most conservatives date this official "war" on the black community from the mid-1980s, launched by President Reagan.[212] With blacks being arrested and confined out of line with their use or sale of drugs, mass incarceration of blacks has been practiced as national policy.[213]

> Mass incarceration is beyond the pale of a society simple constraining crime. It is a vehicle used to further exploit and disempower the black community's....: "When any state system of punishment grows huge and singles out racial or ethnic minorities, it must be considered in different terms than just meting out individual punishment for individual crimes. The unprecedented scale of the imprisonment in the United States in the last quarter of the 20th century, and the multiple injuries this has imposed upon so many of our communities calls for a new understanding of the use of incarceration itself.[214]

The onset of this war on drugs is all the more suspect when America has a dual system of justice for the indictment of black and white drug trafficking. "Nationally, African-Americans are arrested, prosecuted, and imprisoned for drug offenses at far higher rates than whites. This racial disparity bears little relationship to racial differences in drug offending."[215] Figures show that blacks are estimated to be 13 percent of all monthly drug users, but represent 35 percent of arrests for drug possession, 55 percent of convictions, and 74 percent of drug-related prison sentences.[216]

Black men were sent to prison on drug charges at rates ranging from twenty to fifty-seven times those of white men. It seems the system has, in fact, been geared towards incarcerating African Americans. Although Blacks account for only 12 percent of the U.S. population, 44 percent of all prisoners in the United States are Black.[217]

Most critics of this discriminatory trend question arrest practices, mandatory sentencing for the possession of small amounts of drugs, the three strikes laws, and reductions in the availability of parole or early release. With the end result, prisons are crowding with black-and brown-skinned people in record numbers; many first time and non-violent offenders are arrested for drug crimes and prosecuted under mandatory sentencing.

In addition while somewhat dated, but I'm confident the odds have little changed in favor of African American youth. In the 2000 *Chicago Daily Law Bulletin*, the following statistics exposed the hidden preferences inherent in the judiciary system: "Whites account for 71 percent of all juvenile arrests, but only 53 percent of those detained, 50 percent of those tried as adults, and only 25 percent of those sent to adult prison."[218] Compare that to black youths who make up 15 percent of those below the age of 18, they account for 26 percent of arrests, 31 percent of court referrals, 44 percent of those detained pending trial; 46 percent of these youth are waived to adult court, and 58 percent of those sent to adult prison.[219] Be crystal clear, if such disproportionate statistics commentaried the social death of young white males through incarceration or homicide, priorities would shift radically. Society would come to a screeching halt, and this nation would hasten to declare a judicial crisis to protect its national preserve.

What becomes evident is that every effort is made to prevent white youth from ever stepping foot in criminal court. Quite obviously, white youth are the recipients of a status quo favoritism by dispensing reduced sentences through referral to private or community agencies for drug treatment or community service. Unlike black youth, channeled through the judicial process to be prosecuted to the fullest extent of the law for their crimes, the deeper white youth find themselves in the system, the greater is the effort expended to halt their downward plunge. The presumption of white innocence operates from the privileged perspective that they do not belong locked up in a crowded cage. In 2001, a black manchild born that year had an almost one in three chance of going to prison; for a white male child, fewer than six percent.[220]

> Although youth of all races sell and use drugs at similar rates, but African American youth represent 60-75 percent of drug arrests today.[221]

Media Criminalization: "Bad Boy, Whatchua Gonna Do"

The "bad boy" spectacle, sensationalized by the media, lobbies public support for draconian policies against black youth. Season after season, popular cop series crop up like the earlier ones: *America's Most Wanted, Rescue 911, Highway Patrol, LAPD, Law & Order, Cops*; and more recent ones are: *Patrol New York, NYPD, Jail*, the *True Crime* video game. "Bad boy, bad boy, whatchua gonna do when they come for you?" To rack up ratings by playing to fears of black urban "criminality," such series are exploding exponentially. What they accomplish adeptly is to saturate the public faith with an attending callousness about black male life. The handcuffed "bad boy" visceral, dark image intimidates the public with fears of black criminality and his purported, innate human depravity or "super predator" status, until such bigotry is accepted as bone-chillingly normal. A telling commentary of this: "Hollywood's depiction of nonwhites remains less than flattering. The long-running *Cops*, for example, criminalizes blacks, Latinos, and poor white trash nightly on TV." These sensationalized, visual messages terrorize the public into supporting, if not dictating, policies for more U.S. jails and prisons.

Inflaming the public passion with images of black "criminality" endorses an erroneous belief that manchildren's incarceration occurs solely by the hands of their own irascible "nature"—not because they are prisoners of undeclared drug wars. Unlike with slavery, which was inflicted upon black people against our will, prisons say black youth deserve it, that their behavior is asking for it, to be incarcerated, that is, simply because they have done it to themselves. No moral stain is on society's conscience, simply the languishing black forgotten soul.

The Prison Industrial Complex

The manchild's expulsion from society due to this mass black round-up (incarceration) resembles the original penal experience of human beings banished from the Garden of Eden. But even God repented and offered salvific rehabilitation. Despite the grand pledge of allegiance of one nation under God, if the truth be told, this nation is not the city of God, nor does it act like a close approximation. A haven for religious freedom is not all America's history boasts. Sadly, its present march to incarcerate reminisces a return to the penal roots of this nation's humble beginnings.

In the 1600's, England's stagnant economy ceased to adequately handle the material needs of its runaway population, resulting in a high criminal population due to inflationary unemployment and poverty-infested conditions. The poor were unfairly penalized by the onset of these harsh conditions. And with little recourse to improve their station in life, they were often the victims of the hangman's noose as penance for their crimes—often for something as trivial as the theft of a loaf of bread. To address the matter in a supposedly humane fashion, as well as for the sake of economic expediency—never mind empire expansion—England resolved to send a significant number of its criminal "elements" as indentured servants to the American colonies, who were to work off their debt to society under a growing aristocracy of English settlers. Upon completion of their term of service, they were to be granted release.

A different scenario of the imprisonment of blacks and the poor unfolds today, but is still driven by the feverish machinations of economic expediency. With the all but complete outsourcing of its industrial arm to countries traditionally branded the "Third World," there has been a substantial collapse of the U.S. blue-collar sector. With a downsized economy turned technocratic and service-related, the U.S. is grasping at any viable "straw" to revitalize jobs and employment opportunities for blue-collar workers. At such a time, prisons fill the niche and are hailed as an industry match.

With a major shift to the prison industrial complex as the U.S. growth industry of "choice" in the dawning of the twenty-first century, prison human rights organizations are suspicious about the building of so many prisons whether furnishing them with human beings will rank on the order of a self-fulfilling prophecy. More people will be criminalized to accommodate the economic space. And guess upon whom the lash will fall the heaviest? Against whom will the draw of this cursed lot discriminate? To date, all the evidence indicates that the pool will be drawn from poor black and Hispanic communities, out of proportion to our numbers in the general population.[222] A race of people returns to the shackles and the ornaments of captivity, especially with the brisk deployment of "three strikes, you're out" legislation.[223] If not by intent, then by result, issued forth is a seditious mandate for prison administrators to go forth and multiply. Black bodies return to balance sheets of assets and debits, human entries in ledgers of profits and losses, just a short leap from chattel property. But a similar kind of property relationship has unfolded, much like in chattel slavery, where black males resume wearing the shackles and chains of bygone days to announce their status as owned, self-dispossessed, and disenfranchised, with only the slightest difference pronounced by the "moral" defenders of the prison way: "He did it to himself." Problematically, prisons answer that ancient riddle of what to do with black men. Given its voracious appetite for black destinies, the prison industrial complex could prove to be the black community's worst case scenario since slavery.

For white blue-collar communities, prospective prison jobs will boost their flailing economy, raided by corporate down-sizing and factory closings. But conversely, it produces a loyalty to keeping the blood-cycle going, with the promise of lucrative salaries, massive overtime, early retirement, assured pensions, and the old fashioned maintenance of that elusive American middle-class lifestyle. This only recycles a new kind of plantation with the same old kind of conservative economic guard and politics of exploitation.

With the growing shift of prison ownership from state- or government-controlled agencies into the hands of private investors, without substantial regulatory enforcement or monitoring, unequivocally prisons and prison sites will fast become associated with staggering civil and human rights abuses. In fact, they already are. Given that fickle human nature when it comes down to unregulated greed and the propensity of corporations to abuse absolute power, corruption and human rights abuses can only follow suit. This doomsday narrative is rightly feared in prison privatization. As mentioned elsewhere, economic development and political oppression sponsor a common interest in the vested growth of the prison industrial complex. Mass incarceration facilitates the lethal growth of this new U.S. racial and economic apartheid. Ultimately, the U.S. destiny of superpower status has come with an exorbitant human rights cost.

As history teaches, control of human location has been a central theme in the development of the (western) master's narrative of superpower status (progress). From the Middle Passage to the Trail of Tears, relocation and dislocation inscribed the relation of white supremacy to all people of color, beginning with the Native Americans in this country and black Africans abroad, just to name two racial groups. Let it not be thought otherwise—prisons are decisive relocation camps to house that deplored, disposable population, which has been evacuated from urban centers to accommodate the agendas of containment for the sake of capitalist economic progress. Likewise, as designated neo-concentration camps of oppression, prisons indeed will also erupt into fierce sites of human and political human rights struggles in the coming decades. It matters not the delay, regardless of how long it takes, rest assured the human spirit can only be crushed or crucified for so long before it rises again; for ultimately it obeys no master but its own moral taste of freedom.

Prisoners as Slave-Waged Laborers

Among the prohibitive measures in the making, even as I write, which are being devised for the black incarcerated surely include being set aside for the twenty-first century multinational corporate plantations. Corporate avarice for cheap, or better put, unpaid labor, turns black prisoners into slave-waged laborers—the revisiting of our original condition in America, a capitalist preference. Prisons are the growing corporate labor camps of this nation. As many have subsequently testified, among those who had "paid their debt" to society, "We make Nikes and AT&T telephone parts in prison." Already Wall Street trades prison stock in its stock listing, just as it handled slave markets in centuries past—what would be the difference? Human misery for trade profits! Corrections Corporation of America (CCA), one such entity, trades on the New York and American Stock Exchanges. Corporations are building private prisons, a billion dollar industry. Shareholders make money when prison cells are filled. Capitalism has not grown any more redemptive or moral as a result of time transition. Profits, the bottom line, are still its materialist god. Without the grievance process of worker's rights, with the benefits of unionization withheld, and no pretense at human uplift or rehabilitation, slave-waged labor is what results. Prisons will pit incarcerated labor— "slave-wage labor" might better apply—against free-wage labor, if the past is any indicator. Inexorably, the same old racial guards will govern. "Niggers" working from sunup to sundown is what was assured in the words of once presidential hopeful, Texas ex-Senator Phil Gramm, who bragged to the New Hampshire police about "how tough he'll be if only we make him President. I'll make 'em work 10 hours a day, six days a week...."[224]

Upon re-entry to society, these very same ex-offenders cannot make an honest living or be hired for a decent wage, because of the scarlet thread of felon dogging their frustrated steps. In the state of Illinois, for example, "There are more than 50 job categories that are closed to ex-cons, making it against the law for ex-felons to become barbers, nail technicians, morticians, beauticians and butchers."[225] Consider the opportunities closed to youth and adult ex-offenders returning home, who are seeking employment to begin life anew. Those basic job opportunities roped off from them, show just how severely handicapped any naïve notion of a "fresh start" can be. When all things are considered, any inventory of the present circumstances and conditions that could potentially exploit the vulnerability of once incarcerated black boys and men dramatizes the gaping divide between First-and Third World status within a separate and unequal "one nation under God."

Back to the future, American slavery, Jim Crowism, the holocaust, apartheid, lynching, ethnic cleansing, mass murder, all generally volunteer as historic obituary columns, recording sinister periods when social control went hand-in-hand with genocidal death. Human history has been no secret collaborator. What these gross obituaries bear blood witness to are the crimes committed against humanity, as well as the depths to which human inhumanity can plunge. Some of these happened not so long ago. That "strange fruit," as jazz crooner Billie Holiday eulogizes, is also the blighted harvest of western democracies. From this, black people must take caution and heed respectfully the oracles of history that warn every minority or marginal group to beware when a racial/ethnic group is treated as disease-ridden dependents (such as the high HIV/AIDS rates in the black community), or targeted as socially and economically expendable, or set up racially, on the basis of the politics of inferiority, as exterminable. In due course, the U.S.'s purging of its dark citizens, its native sons, will be less alarmist and crude as, say, a Bosnia or a Rwanda, too squeamish for a liberal democracy, narcissistic about its human right sensibilities, but it will achieve the same end result in the genocidal disposal of unwanted citizens.

"Not Tested on Animals," but Prisoners

Farfetched but not inconceivable, with the black male life-force devalued to the point of disposable, it's not beyond the pale that black male inmates could be pooled for testing as experimental guinea pigs, given our long history in American folklore as the interminable beast. Their human sanctity would not be counted worthy to fall under the holy guarantee, "not tested on animals, no cruelty to animals." What grounds my suspicion that the vulnerability of inmates could come up for exploitation is how the past exposes the gross negligence of the medical establishment in using blacks and the poor to advance medical experimentation, much of it to feather the patent inventories of giant pharmaceutical companies. Claims might be made that past practices in twentieth century U.S. prisons could be a frightening omen of what's to come, with prisons in the hands of unscrupulous profiteering. Possibly, it could be a re-visitation of what was permitted to happen by the world community in the Nazi's World War II concentration camps, like human experimentation at Dachau. Ironically, Jewish Holocaust survivors were liberated from gas chambers, crematories and human experimentation by American soldiers. Only now in this nation, there is the outright collusion among the U.S. medical community, pharmaceutical companies, and the highly controversial U.S. government's Food and Drug Administration (FDA) to disenfranchise prisoners of their human rights in not becoming involuntary "clinical test subjects." Unlike in the case of the Holocaust victims where a fascist state government perpetrated these crimes against humanity, corporate interests are being brokered as social policies of today.

The Tuskegee Experiment is the most notorious. But a lesser known case, though just as egregious, is the U.S. Army contract with the University of Pennsylvania, under the professorial leadership of Dr. Albert Kligman, to conduct clinical testing on human subjects at the maximum security Holmesburg prison.[226] From the 1950s through the mid-1970s, amid the U.S. medical community's moral blackout, black prisoners were overwhelmingly marshaled as human guinea pigs to be utilized to test cosmetics, such as Retin-A to the chemical testing of substances like dioxins, radioactive isotopes, hallucinogenic drugs for military warfare, and injected with malaria, hepatitis and other diseases.[227] Directly or indirectly, Holmesburg Prison provided over 30 major companies and federal agencies open access to clinical trials from experiments carried out on human subjects.[228] Trial testing was perpetrated upon black prisoners, with little else than dubious letters of consent and promises of minimal remuneration, which much of that tallied to commissary credits for cigarettes and such. Lawsuits were filed by the violated, but no compensation can match the profits that Kligman and corporations gained from the gruesome abuses of those who were black and imprisoned— vulnerable. Always, when it comes down to protecting America's nominal citizens like prisoners, looking the other way for the sake of avarice gain portends an everyday fact of life.

In today's materialist culture, many, including the medical community, simply believe inmates should be a handy supply of human subjects for medical trials. So preferred, they're cheaper, with less liability than volunteers from the general population. A report released by the Institutes of Medicine of the National Academy of Sciences, as recently as August 2006, strongly urged the government to loosen current federal restrictions imposed on prisons. This call for laxed regulation is ostensibly so that "inmates" can benefit from clinical trials that would lead to treatment for HIV/AIDS, STDs and other diseases. A well-tested skepticism monitors this as a mercenary call being touted as salvific for "inmates." Linn Washington, Jr. of the *Philadelphia Tribune* weighs in extensively on the issue. His strong reservation toward this push to loosen restrictions is apparent:

> Ironically, this push to relax restrictions involving prisoners who participate in clinical trials follows years during which tens of thousands of AIDS-infected inmates, who either entered prison with AIDS or contracted the deadly disease while incarcerated, were denied access to widely available, already approved medications on the market that not only would have dramatically improved their health, prolonging their lives, but would have also prevented many of the extremely painful and debilitating symptoms that accompany HIV/AIDS.

He further criticizes how decades of conservative policy and red-tape measures under the banner of "public safety" actually aided in undeserving needy prisoners' medical care. So why now is the government supportive of laxed restrictions? is his query.

> If condoms had been allowed to be distributed in prisons all along it could [have] significantly reduced the rampant transmission of HIV within many minority communities across the country, which is directly linked, in part, to the prohibition of condom distribution in prisons.[229]

Although cleverly hailed as a win-win for all by the Institute of Medicine, activists protest such blatant avarice, because they are not beguiled by claims of aid to prisoners, but know that the "real beneficiaries in today's shorter route to Federal Drug Administration (FDA) approval are pharmaceutical companies."[230] Paul Wright, editor of *Prison Legal News*, puts the matter succinctly, "It strikes me as pretty ridiculous to start talking about prisoners getting access to cutting-edge research and medications when they can't even get penicillin and high-blood-pressure pills. I have to imagine there are larger financial motivations here."[231] His suspicions are probably correct. Victimization by the unscrupulous ethics of the medical community in conducting illicit clinical trials on prisoners and the poor throughout this nation has yet to be fully prosecuted in favor of its multitude of victims. This readily answers the attacks of why prisoners must stay vigilant to the point of scrutinizing any so-called "benefit" research crusade. With prisoners being the most socially vulnerable, they are ripe for plucking—exploitation, coercion, manipulation, deceit—incurring the least amount of public outrage. Just generally, prisoners are so desired because they are hidden inside thick walls where the media and public scrutiny do not penetrate at will.

In the Holmesburg case, whether on the part of an Ivy League educational institution, the U.S. government, the medical profession, or pharmaceutical companies, corporate and institutional collusion profited at the expense of vulnerable black prisoners. They were betrayed into human experimentation under the pretext of participating in research and healing. Incidents such as these urge the black community's vigilance as to how prisoners may be given another dubious disclaimer to sign as consent, with a life sentence "reduced" as compensation. Protocols of protection, as every scientist knows, are only as good as their enforcement.

Finally, others wish that the black community would "just get over it"—its suspicion and cynicism about the medical community's complicity and past atrocities of prisons as death camps. Only the very privileged can boast such a cavalier attitude, never having been hapless preys of unjust bureaucracy, but poised to be the avaricious beneficiaries of profiteering enterprises such as this. For the rest of us, these historical atrocities are a constant indictment of and act as living memories of what happens when absolute power can be wielded over the lives of the socially vulnerable. Always those twentieth century tragedies are still so close at hand and recent to early twenty-first century family members. The ripples are still being felt in detrimental ways.

On the other hand, prisoners could, of course, supply the manpower for a reserve fighting force. Attracting uncoerced U.S citizens to fight unjust wars has become increasingly unpopular. And the old gimmicks of "be all you can be" no longer sell. Naturally, the middle- and upper middle-classes will not draft their young sons and daughters for tours of "dishonorable" duty. Only a handful of sons and daughters of Congressmen and women are fighting in Iraq now, according to the most recent poll. Without the re-enactment of the draft, then, if not the poor and working-class, who will go? How puzzling that black criminality can be rehabilitated into a squad of mercenary soldiers, but not model citizens?[232] Even as I write, what recently drew controversial public ire was the use of untrained civilians as "soldiers for hire" in the Iraq war. In a growing climate of recruiting outside of traditional "be all you can be" channels, private armies are being sponsored by the U.S. government under the paperwork disguises of subcontractors. Blackwater CEO Erik Prince had to testify before the House Committee on Oversight and Government Reform to explain the mercenaries' war crimes of his company against Iraqi citizens.[233] Sure to follow will be citizenship for hire (service).[234] But the pending question is, how will the black community respond to a new set of abolitionist politics? with a Sanctuary Movement. A reactivated Underground network? Can we resist the call to salvage our broken brothers' lives? A significant percentage of the national population cannot be incarcerated, without also incarcerating the country, as well, and putting it on guard.

🏠🏠🏠

An "Abolitionist" Freedom Movement

Converted into a strategic resistance movement is what must be done with that wanton shame and guilt, borne as a rugged cross—much of which the black community flagellates itself with—because husbands, sons, partners, brothers, uncles, fathers, cousins are fraternals of the incarcerated. When incarceration is practiced as national policy upon the black community—what else could it be?—it should be denounced as a democratic heresy. Whether we admit it or not, the African American community is a community under siege. Every church or community center, I am convinced, should have a kente scroll on reverent display, naming the lives that have been lost to the anonymity and animosity of these growing statistics, behind security bars at Attica, Riker's Island, Sing Sing, San Quentin, or Lorton. These national prisoners' lives should be posted high and low, adorned with memorial symbolism, and lit with our holy rage until this massacre of black talent has been rescinded. Here could begin the seedlings of an artistic political movement for those incarcerated. The black church, or any black religious institution or movement naming itself relevant to this new freedom cause, should shoulder some of this responsibility of ritualizing the memory of this historical phase of the black community's resistance to forces of domination, particularly if it seeks to stay meaningful in a twenty-first century religious marketplace.

All too often, sermons and speeches of black powerlessness are spouted from the pulpits and podiums by ordained and elected representatives in the black community. Any such anointing of black powerlessness is frightening in its potential to condition black life to adopt such a fraudulent belief, and can be emotionally addictive to an "at-risk" people. If I had the choice, rather than preaching powerlessness, I would configure black historic and contemporary community experience as persecuted. Let me explain why. Persecuted directly relates to how young black males are targeted for harassment, death, or "luckily," an incarcerated status. In certain age groups, our young black men have a better chance of going to jail than college. Since 1995 to the present time, one in every three young black males lives out his life as a ward of the legal justice system. In some major urban centers, the numbers climb as high as one in every five black males. Black inmates between the ages of 17 and 26 make up a whopping forty percent.[235] Most arresting is that African Americans under 18 comprise 15 percent of their national age group, yet 26 percent of them represent the arrest rates. In all, "blacks make up 43.9 percent of the state and federal prison populations but only 12.3 percent of the U.S. population."[236] Another way of looking at the broad picture, while only 6 percent of the United States population, African American males total almost 40 percent of the prison population.[237] How are black people to receive this slow but sure decimation of the black community, stealing our young warriors in their youth and young adult prime?

After the Wilmington 12, and the Scottsboro Boys, after decades of lynching, vigilante justice, and chattel status—after all this, black male prisoners return to less than 3/5 of a constitutional constituent.[238] Due to felony convictions, 1.46 million black men out of a total voting population of 10.4 million have become disenfranchised.[239] With over one million black males having had some contact with the criminal justice system and a marked growth in black females behind bars, many of these people can only be considered political prisoners—this tireless growth of detainees as a matter of national policy. Indeed, how else can their systematic imprisonment be described as anything other than a state of persecution? How else are we to interpret this great exodus from our community, with no North Star to guide them to their human fulfillment?

Therefore, the word "persecuted" conjures up a different image of this repressive state of affairs plaguing the black community. It evokes in the black public mind a radically different social understanding of our collective self that is less passive and more redemptive, proactive. "Persecuted" inspires our moral identity as a community of resisters to oppression, unjust laws, corporate ruling entities, or political powers-that-be. Take your political and ideological pick. But "persecuted" secures the noble quest to still press on and fight. Its image, thereof, can create a unity for social action, for the idea of persecution puts us on the moral defense rather than cowering to passive submission. Closely synonymous with legitimate claims of injustice, "persecuted" judges that there is wrong-doing on the part of another. It keeps the borders clear as to who or what is the enemy. Perhaps, I have no right to beg for such simplistic demarcations of friend and foe in a global world order. But to do nothing because of the inescapable political complication is a worse sin.

Conversely, powerlessness denotes that the battle is already won and defeat is a foregone conclusion. When we think of our lives as powerless, it sounds a death toll, a shackle that chains any sense of bodily freedom, the removal of agency. Powerlessness images the black community as weak, feeble, unable to resist, not empowered. Unfortunately, that strong lobby in black powerlessness has so galvanized the black race into a self-fulfilling prophecy of paralyzing apathy, drug addiction, denial, and a raging self-hatred. Every chant of black powerlessness will resonate in our disempowerment as a collective, until we cannot resist physical, economic, political, and social incarceration. Any community thought powerless only waits uneasily for the death toll of its own demise. Who has filled our minds with such a defective belief in our own black body politic? A fresh canon of Scriptures needs to be written upon our hearts and minds, which inspires an active, uncensored, infallible, faithful belief in the power of our own black body politic.

CHAPTER 8

On the Anniversary Eve of the Death of Amadou Diallo
The Tale of Two Cities

Most of the craziest and most deranged people in the world were white. People like Dahmer, Bundy, Sam, the kids from Columbine, Manson, heck Bobbet, Harding and the list goes on. White people do the most extreme things, period, and we get damn near all the heat for it. Why is it that we haven't heard of a white man being beaten and having a plunger stuck up his butt or cops letting 40 plus shots at a white person. Let's leave the subject of cops for a second, blacks/latinos haven't hung a white person in Mexico or in New York, but yet the cops don't go harassing white people.

Carlos Minter, Medgar Evers College student

At the doorstep of his Bronx apartment, Amadou Diallo, a West African immigrant, another devout supplicant of the American dream, met its nightmare head-on, gunned down in a wild-west shootout by four of New York's "finest" (NYPD). With that "madd" rush of forty shots, 19 marked the bullseye, Diallo, that is, protected by little else than a jacket wallet thought to be a gun clasped in his hand. Tragically, Diallo died not knowing what sin he had committed, other than being black, alive, and in the wrong place at the wrong time, even though his doorsteps said home—the irony of it all. Looking for a rapist, the cops stumbled upon an innocent, unarmed man—black though. Forty shots volunteered, "He'll do." NYPD was in the neighborhood investigating a rape case.[240] However, historical precedence was not on Diallo's side; for any public outcry for the unlynched black rapist has always been a vigilante defense for extreme measures, without a pretense of attention to the "messy" details of civil rights. The lynching of blacks is a historical practice that ceases to die. Now, it's done New York City style.

On the Eve of the Death of Amadou Diallo

On the eve of the 5th anniversary of the death of Amadou Diallo, Brooklyn heard another mad, death-shot ring out on the rooftop of Louis Armstrong Houses, and another black youth, Timothy Stansbury fell dead, the victim of another unjustified homicide. On a routine patrol, an NYPD cop happened upon the silhouette of a male. And because it was in one of Brooklyn's housing projects, because it was dark and on forbidden territory, the rooftop, he had to be black, blazing, threatening, and unwielding, a menace to society, and bent upon jeopardizing a cop's security. Of course, he had to have an imagined gun, if not the authentic shooter. With pistol drawn, any cop shooting blindly in an urban housing project is sure to hit the intended target to be, execute another black male youth. So the cop reflexes with a shot from his pistol, down goes another black male with a CD defense in his hand, unlike a wallet or a gun.

Timothy Stansbury's and Amadou Diallo's unforgiven deaths are not simply the fated tale of two cities—two New York City boroughs, to be exact, Brooklyn and the Bronx. Their death are the manchild's tale throughout all of America, wherever his shadow darkens. This is the way, the only way, Diallo's death was commemorated Brooklyn-style, only he had an inept wallet to armor him from the weapons of death, a rush of forty bullets, that is. One death in the "gathering" pot of an immigrant community in the Bronx, another across the bridge in Brooklyn's Louis Armstrong housing project, is this where similarities meet, and being in the "wrong" place at the wrong time never ends for black males?

What I found particularly difficult to reconcile is that Stansbury is being blamed for his own death, as cross-examined by the shot of the cop: Why was he up there? Who told him he could take to the roof? Had he a right to assume he had the choice to be free? Didn't his mother advise him of his lost protection unique to his black birth, a guarantor of invisibility—where there is no rightful place where his safety is ever secure? Such queries rudely accuse young black men of being careless with their lives because they choose to be public, free and unaccosted. Blamed for being young, blamed for being black, blamed for being male, blamed for being at-risk, and taking a short-cut to death. But unbeknownst to him was that his life had already been forfeited when he took it into his hands and made it public. For black and brown brothers to choose visibility is always to star in a uniquely American tragedy: he killed himself for living, breathing— what the heck—being alive; a walking "suicide" makes him a volunteer death candidate in the eyes of some uniformed beholders.[241]

"Owning" any humanity at all puts them at extreme risk for execution. That old, old ritual of protection by shuffling submission and invisibility, once adopted for survival's sake, is now rejected on principle by black and brown young male descendents who crave the manhood of visibility and self-possession, props won by civil rights campaigns. And yet every generation of manchildren chances that unchanced reality: "It could have happened to me." Although the names may be tailored to adapt to a modern world milieu, whether it's the ex-Ku Klux Klan, ex-white paddy riders, the badge toting uniformed blue and gray, still they reside as the black male natural-born predator. Indoctrinated into the irrational fears of a racist psyche is the death of the black and brown male by "any means necessary." The western narrative of the survival of the "white" fittest is alive and well, and just as brutal as any rogue nation.

From the cop's perspective, anybody who would be on the rooftop is probably suspect and guilty of mischief and foul play, indeed 911 dangerous; then being on the alert requires weapon protection, drawn for a ready kill, because it isn't safe to be caught off guard. This growing New York trend of victim bloodsport, cops seeking prey (trouble) instead of posturing themselves as a deterrent to trouble— permits no margin of error for youthful horseplay, taking a night stroll, checking out the scenery, certainly not a shortcut for innocuous CDs. It will and must forfeit black male life.

Is that how we explain the bloodsport lynching of every James Byrd,[242] according to conservative opinion, of being in the wrong place at the wrong time? If that be so, where then is the right place ever for a black man in America? Who dares to name it? Where can it be found? Hell?

🏛🏛🏛

CHAPTER 9

Cosby's Ambivalent Black Community
"It Still Takes a 'Village'"

To me young people come first, they have the courage where we fail And if I can but shed some light as they carry us through the gale, The older I get the better I know that the secret of my going on, Is when the reins are in the hands of the young, who dare to run against the storm, Not needing to clutch for power, not needing the light just to shine on me, I need to be one in the number as we stand against tyranny, Struggling myself don't mean a whole lot, I've come to realize, That teaching others to stand up and fight is the only way my struggle survives.

Sweet Honey In the Rock

With all the controversy, it is easy to forget the words of thanks and praise in Bill Cosby's speech celebrating the fiftieth anniversary of the Brown decision. He called out the names of civil rights activists who worked on the Brown case: NAACP lawyers; the psychologist Kenneth Clark; the head of the National Council of Negro Women, Dorothy Height. Cosby praised young black people of that era who "marched and were hit in the face with rocks," especially the Little Rock Nine, who faced angry mobs to get into a high school that remained segregated even after Brown was the law.

Juan Williams, *Enough*

At the National Association of the Advancement of Colored People (NAACP) commemorative event for the 50th Anniversary of *Brown v. the Board of Education*, entertainer, philanthropist and educator Bill Cosby trumpeted a tough-love wake-up call that struck a touchy chord in certain sectors of the black community. His speech, in fact, left not a few bent out of shape with his considerable recitation of escalating teen pregnancy, disappearing dads, 50 percent dropout rate in minority schools, parents buying expensive sneakers for a child who can't read, and just generally the moral scourging of the values of black youth, if not poor, black people, in full public view. Bucking centuries-old precedence about not airing dirty laundry in public for fear of further tarnishing the black community's image in white company, Cosby cast off the conservative restraint and broadcast his high-profile moral crusade in full view of the naked public's eye: during the commemorative event, in debates, and at radio and newspaper interviews. Even if Cosby had taken the less visible route and simply took it to the black streets, incurring less ire was not an assured certainty either. No longer swept under the carpet out of public view, his diatribe exposed the crisis-proportion of the conditions decimating the lives and opportunities of black youth, as well as embroiling the black community in an "underachieving" culture. Cosby is worried about the black community's ability to remain viable to compete in a twenty-first century global economy. At its best, as expressed in his speech, Cosby's disillusionment raised the stakes about the level of intervention necessary to turn the hip hop generation around. His alarm alerts us all to the fact that business as usual will not secure tangible hope for that disposable generation.

The Cosby's Great Debate

Cosby, most visible and vocal, answers the present crisis in the black community with a charge of lack of personal responsibility. His reprimand dispenses with old excuses; he has grown tired of black people using racism as a painless excuse for past and current failures.[243] In the home is where Cosby takes critical aim. He blames parents for not taking seriously their responsibility to mother and father their children; In his opinion, handling their parental authority in irresponsible ways has produced the present epic crisis. Rather than give their children moral guidance, they have settled for a confusing, materialist friendship. As his words accuse:

These people are not parenting. They are buying
things for their kids - $500 sneakers for what?
And won't spend $200 for 'Hooked on Phonics.'
Everybody knows it's important to speak English
except these knuckleheads. You can't be a doctor
with that kind of crap coming out of your
mouth.[244]

Parents of today, according to Cosby, are in the
unenviable position of buying the love of their children,
something once merited as sacred regard between parent and
child. In his view, that has led to a destructive malaise where
some parents have woefully, and others willfully, neglected or
just generally abdicated that all critically important personal
responsibility, parenting. As a tragic consequence, children have
lost their moral compass. Unlike the pre-sixties years, children,
for instance, no longer have any moral shame about what they
do. They get "pregnant" or "locked-up," but dare a reprimand
from parents. In view of his own cherished moral values
bestowed by the black community, those bygone days of dignity
and pride, he assesses that the present-day moral dereliction
knows no moral bound. Generally, Cosby mourns the loss of
dignity among black people as a people.[245]
No matter how reactionary Cosby's moral crusading
might appear to some black people, few would disagree that
Cosby is rightly arguing that there is a fine line to which black
people can and should blame all of our problems on skin color.
His actual words, "In all of this work we can not blame white
people."[246] Cosby knows that black skin is no new trial to the
black community. He bears the racial stripes, as one who was
groomed in that historical crucible as a race man. With pride,
he, and others like him, bore the racial weight of a peopleness
without complaint. Knowing that in white eyes, there is rarely
the black individual. "They all look alike," was the pejorative
joiner to "being alike." Starting out in his career, for certain, he
was representing "all blacks" if he failed or "exceptional" if by
perchance he succeeded. Overcoming that divided interest
against his people, from a career perspective, Cosby navigated
well the crushing weight, the demeaning blows, of being

measured by the yardstick of a peopleness but triumphed into a "special" individual. Yet he never forgot his roots, as he could've done quite easily, like so many others. Friends and foes acknowledge Cosby's unflagging philanthropist commitment to the Civil Rights Movement. Day-in and day-out, balancing that act between peopleness and being counted as an individual, he did not demur; nor did he wallow in the seduction of racial victimhood, but shouldered his race obligations proudly, if not pridefully, in the white public's eye. Rightly so, one gains the impression that trench warfare is nothing new to him. From his personal experience of being on the firing line as a race representative—his choice or not, his black skin recruited him. Cosby's life story testifies that black achievement only came with a mighty struggle. And as he looked around him at the lost condition of our black youth and their parent generation, his outraged reaction decried the fact that the collateral of black history had been badly squandered, mishandled by its beneficiaries. Understandable he felt called upon to chastise his people, to warn them that the hour of accountability was near, and that the good-will of race men and women like himself was nigh exhausted from a struggle that younger brothers and sisters of today seemed to care little about anyway. From his heartfelt perspective, Cosby is really decrying the poor not holding up their "end of the bargain" that others paid dearly for like Kenneth Clarks, the Little Rock Nine, and Linda Brown to give succeeding generation a fighting chance, which in their time, they could only merit as a dream deferred.

Against this historical memory, Rev. Jesse Jackson, more moderate in tone, weighs in:

> There is no real debate in the Black community concerning personal responsibility. It is well settled that while institutional inequality and injustice are real, they never excuse doing less than one's best to overcome the effects. Certainly, Blacks and the poor face structural inequality. Cosby argues that while it may not be the fault of blacks for being in poverty, it is our burden to challenge and break out of it.[247]

Even as someone like Reverend Jesse Jackson extends deference to the hard-earned racial stripes of Cosby, others claim a less benign perspective about his public pulpit. Milwaukee Journal Sentinel columnist Eugene Kane, also born in North Philadelphia and attended Temple University like Cosby, had this to say: "Given his record as a philanthropist who had donated millions to black colleges and black causes in general, Cosby has certainly earned the right to speak his mind." At the same time, he chides Cosby's grand generalization in its unfair diminishment of black life only.

> Still, there's a sense of uneasiness whenever somebody like Cosby uses the same language some whites use to justify their racism.... Particularly, the idea that poor blacks and their children weigh down the rest of society, or that every black person behind bars deserves to be incarcerated. Sure, some blacks may fit that description, not all. Some white people, too.[248]

(In truth, some of Cosby's language does reminisce the preaching of neoconservatives like William Bennett, one who calls for a radical public policy initiative—abort black babies to reduce their so-called bastardy drain on society's resources.) While Cosby's criticism of the black poor might be received with mixed feelings in the words of Kane, Reverend Jesse Jackson concurs that it is the black community's burden to challenge structural inequality and break free of its debilitating hold on black life. Prolific as always, he captures Cosby's sentiment but with less of a victim-blaming fervor. His words of admonition could have been uttered decades ago. They reiterate that although obstacles of yesteryears still plague the black community, yet they remain our responsibility to overcome. We are still held accountable to be agents of social change, is what Jackson urges.

If the playing field is uneven, those who succeed
and benefit most from the struggle of others are
not the ones who makes it even. It is always the
victims of the uneven playing field who must
rise up and make it even—that's the legacy of
our civil rights struggle: Not blaming the victim,
but securing social responsibility.[249]

Less diplomatic in his attack upon Cosby's tirade, public
intellectual Michael Eric Dyson has emerged in this debate as
one of his arch-opponents. Taking out his sling to tackle this
Goliath head-on, he does a hard-core read of Cosby's
professional and personal life in his infinitely popular, *Is Bill
Cosby Right? Or Has the Black Middle-Class Lost Its Mind?*
Stone by stone, Dyson chips away at the mystification slicked
to Cosby's personality as America's favorite Dad to reveal a
less than savory saint. What Dyson accomplishes in his
dissection as well as less-savory exposé of Cosby's moral
failings, I'm not quite sure—other than perhaps to demystify
the legitimacy of the messenger. In so doing, he shifts the
attention from some of our moral failings as a people to the
individual failings of Cosby. But after all is said and done in *Is
Bill Cosby Right?* sectors of black America are, in fact, being
rounded up for jails and prison bins. The untamed drop-out
rates are soaring—even if they are less than 50 percent as Dyson
charges. Teen pregnancy condemns black children to poverty.
And the lack of preparation of our youth to claim a competitive
future, with all the social impediments they face today, only
ensures that they will lag behind in the global job market. On
the other side, to be fair to Dyson, he worries that Cosby's
demonization of poor, black people and their children will
redound to their further vulnerability with tragically unweighed
consequence, especially as he notes the neoconservatives and
naysayers fawning all over Cosby to congratulate him on taking
the "color-blind" leap in making his diatribe against the black

poor public. Dyson says as much: "Cosby's rabid insistence on personal responsibility to the exclusion of every other variety of responsibility has predictably won him plaudits from black and white conservatives…. He fears Cosby is giving less than sympathetic critics a pass to disparage black people at will, and explains it in these terms:

> Cosby's insistence on self-help lets society off the hook, including governmental bodies, segments of private industry and certainly racist quarters of the culture that have like vultures picked at the bones of the black suffering that they, or their ideological predecessors, helped to impose. It is intellectually irresponsible for Cosby to spout his gospel of self-help and personal responsibility without paying strict attention to the social forces that have pulverized the black families he now attacks in terms that are, he unapologetically admits, "vulgar."[251]

But for sure, after the fray of a Cosby-Dyson's smoking duel, black youth are still in desperate need of mentors like Dyson and Cosby, both fallible humanity, with marks of feebleness staining each unchaste past, but committed to the liberating best in a peopleness.

"The Truly Disadvantaged"

Cosby does not look to institutional measures to remedy the crisis in black America, somehow he communicates that their work was done with the approval of *Brown*. He expresses it succinctly, *"Brown versus the Board of Education* is no longer the white person's problem. We have got to take the neighborhood back."[252] Yet, can the plight of the black poor be shouldered by the derelictions of personal responsibility alone? as Cosby chastises. Renowned sociologist William J. Wilson penetrates to the heart of the matter, linking the present conditions of the black poor not only to an economically depressed landscape, but also the moral failure of the black middle class to its lesser well-off sisters and brothers. Noticeably absent is this perspective in Cosby's present-day platform, but necessary to generously inform his politics. Decades prior, say as early as the seventies, Wilson spotted some disturbing trends that would prove detrimental to the black community's economic viability and autonomy. In his book, *The Truly Disadvantaged*, the argument Wilson renders spells out in deliberate terms some of the causal conditions that deserve critical assessment in a blame-it-on personal responsibility social and political climate. His reasoning hinges upon the exodus of middle-and working-class families from ghetto neighborhoods. According to him, this untimely exodus removed important "social buffers" that had the potential to "deflect the full impact of the kind of prolonged and increasing joblessness that plunged inner-city neighborhoods in the 1970s and early 1980 into joblessness, created by uneven economic growth and periodic recessions."[253] His argument, quite simple, in effect, is that intact community institutions would have staved off elements of the social disintegration by absorbing some of the social shock inevitably produced by a shifting economic context with joblessness as its harmful fallout.

> This argument is based on the assumption that even if the truly disadvantaged segments of an inner-city area experience a significant increase in long-term spells of joblessness, the basic institutions in that area (churches, schools, stores, recreational facilities, etc.) would remain viable if much of the base of their support comes from the more economically stable and secure families.[254]

Though his position on race is contested on many fronts, the revealing research of Wilson supports some of Dyson's own contention on the matter and confirms name-calling is not enough to remedy the pervasive problems facing black America. The need for social buffers to stem the tide of black despair and misery is just as necessary now as it ever was. This means not a great deal of preaching about black youth failure, but where are we strategically located in the lives of these disadvantaged, young people to intervene[255] into their isolationism with guidance and positive role modeling?

From Wilson's research, the exodus of the black middle-class has only exacerbated conditions of social isolation. How do we change that tide? To my mind, for instance, that's why the network of the black church emerges as an ever more significant institution for leveling class lines and uniting the black community. Given its anchor position historically in the community and its mission to reach all regardless of social status, it possesses the natural ability to bring the welfare recipient and the teacher together, the underachieving children and the overachievers, a stratification of different classes singing and praying together. That is one of the enduring legacies of the black church to black survival and posterity. But the church can't do it alone. Wilson never said it would. *Crisis in the Village*, a well-written piece by Christian ethicist Robert Franklin, now president of the historic Morehouse College, calls everybody accountable.[256] He examines all the anchor institutions in the black community—the church, the family, and black colleges. Why Franklin didn't include traditional civil rights organizations. Also, in Franklin's work is puzzling. To his credit, journalist Juan Williams does some of that painful dissection in *Enough*. Not a kind commentary, he follows the trail of Cosby's argument to indict the "poverty-pimping" role of traditional civil rights organizations. Also, in Franklin's own work, the telling absence of community-based organizations as post-sixties' anchors, now pivotal in the solution to this moral crisis, was most curious. Celebrities like Denzel Washington and others credit the mentoring work of organizations like the Boys and Girls Clubs for salvaging their uncertain lives and anchoring hope. For those many shunning the doors of the church, community-based organizations took them in to mentor them into their human possibility. As important as Franklin's anchor institutions are, to a certain degree, community-based organizations remind us, as Dyson has done so eloquently, that elitist institutions are not where the black poor might feel the most welcome or will necessarily seek out a helping hand, but organizations that encourage an equality of acceptance and respect. "Everybody is somebody here." Does the black church still obey and embody that Golden Rule?

As to Franklin's task, he pointedly assesses the brokenness of those anchor institutions for the purpose of rethinking their mission for a twenty-first century community in crisis. He comes back to: "It still takes a village." For good measures, his book doesn't end on just a descriptive note; he actually designs strategies for "renewing the village."[257] The final point made is what the black community has known since its birth in America: that these are difficult times; not times to give up or give in to the luxury of despair, but to keep marching up the freedom highway, even if in the process the sacrifice one makes on behalf of our downtrodden youth generation never surfaces to the light of day, just doing it is its own recompense, as W.E.B. Dubois prophetically urged, on behalf of "strangers, unborn babes, uncreated worlds." It is the cost of community, of being human, and more significantly, claims of making a difference. This is the unsolicited legacy of those who care.

The "Afristocracy" vs the "Ghettocracy"

In what social critic Dyson maligns as the coldhearted Afristocracy in[258] hot pursuit of the American materialist dream, chased almost fetishly as a sacred grail by some, left behind is that other overly "disparaged" camp, the Ghettocracy.[259] In his opinion, the mantra of the black middle-class has never been more like that perky Jefferson's theme song, "Movin' on up," away from that other black America. As a result, in that other

America, with so few Norman Lear's *Good Times* moments to sweeten the bland, bitter taste of poverty, too many manchildren, numbers untold, are sentenced to the squalid holds of inner-city crime and decay, faces truly trapped at the bottom of a well.[260] From their mounting casualties, there can be little doubt that hope on their part is waning, being replaced by a coldhearted fatalism. At all of sixteen, manchildren cynically advise one another, "We all got to go sometime." Tomorrows are failing them. Just to grasp how pervasive the limits are that menace the manchildren's future ad infinitum, according to one rapper, the slim pickings facing him in the urban job market are either "slingin' crack rock or you got a wicked jump shot."[261] Their American dream is slipping away.

In the tragic end, can there be any reasonable explanation to our languishing manchildren, those conflicted souls, why so many of the Afristocracy have aspired to be free of them in their our own anxious urban flight and middle-class arrogance? when their very "hood" and class history hail some of them as their very own "homeboy and girl" and testify from whence they have sprung, with little wish to return.[262] In truth, not enough of Afristocracy have remained involved, at least, long enough to mentor and role model righteous values for manchildren, to suffer with them in the messy trenches of their difficult lives, and ultimately, to intervene compassionately to save them from this suicidal path that raps: "I expect to die young." Who is there to remind them that "you are somebody" is more than an overused rallying cry, but a divine state of being? All rhetoric with little substance makes the Afristocracy hypocrites. As one youth righteously accuses: "How can you see a future when there is a black teen shot or killed every day? It (is) easy for some to say, 'keep hope alive' when they're not dealing with the problems that we the people who live in the inner city have to deal with."[263] Is it any wonder that manchildren hemorrhage so much rage, when the outrageous fortune of "poverty and pain" are the "cornerstones" of their very stolen lives? And where is Cosby's ambivalent black community?

①②⑦

So, while the black community continues to laud the gratuitous opportunities brokered by civil rights legislations and protest advocacy, still our manchildren are not saved. The hard-won gains of the Civil Rights revolution have not or did not trickle down far enough to advantage enough poor blacks of that Ghettocracy to stay the execution of disposability—those whom Wilson calls the "truly disadvantaged."

Brown versus Economic Equality

More pointedly, in his speech "Dr. Bill Cosby Speaks," Cosby made quite a stir about the failing drop-out rates among black youth. Since it was the 50th year anniversary celebration of *Brown v. Topeka Board of Education*, who would fault him for focusing upon education? Perhaps, unlike since *Brown*, education has emerged as one of those critical measures of just how far manchildren have fallen behind, and so too the black community's hope of being competitive in a global world. Although a hard-fought and won area of civil rights activism, education has degenerated into one of those sore spots of integration, and shown itself as a most vulnerable beachhead. As articulated in his speech, Cosby found that 50 percent drop-out rate in public schools baffling, as an embarrassment, an affront to *Brown* and its hard-won civil rights struggle. To explain adequately why this institutional casualty is haunting the black community at such an alarming rate calls for a deeper analysis. Author and professor Derrick Bell provides that carefully honed perspective in his work, *Silent Covenant*. He reviews the complexity of *Brown's* failure from the intimacy of practicing as a NAACP civil rights attorney decades ago and as an activist in his own right. From the beginning, Bell sadly admits in *Silent Covenant* the failure of *Brown* to realize all of a people's dream, hooked to its integrationist wagon. The book proceeds to offer substantive insight into one of the tactical weaknesses of *Brown*—racial fortuity is what Bell calls it—to assess why this factor was critical in the success of school segregation being struck down, but an unforeseen failure in achieving racial equality.[264] What is Bell actually charging in assigning *Brown's* success to racial fortuity? And what are we to make of this? Herein is how he actually explains it:

> We hardly noticed that the advances we hailed actually marked those periods when policymakers realized that remedies for racial injustice and the nation's needs coincided. Fortuity was more important than any national commitment to "freedom and justice for all."

Certainly, recent decades have confirmed the ominous truth of Bell's analysis.

Bottom line, though, judicial decisions alone such as *Brown* could not guarantee that much-sought after prize of freedom, opportunity, and social justice without a full commitment on the part of this nation to integration at every level of society. In particular, drawing back from shifting the socioeconomic status quo barred the way to the black community achieving equity in some quite distinct ways. Much of what we see today devastating black youth can be laid at the feet of those very mitigating forces that legal advocates of *Brown* had not expected to contend with or to combat. Bell expounds it.

> While civil rights lawyers worked to remove the most obvious legal symbols of segregation, we left it to A. Philip Randolph and the National Urban League to address the major changes in the economic outlook of a great many black people…. Neither the *Brown* decision nor our efforts to give it meaning had any relevance to the plight of those whom we had not forgotten, but had no real idea how to help.[265]

Decades later, this resulted in some of the scathing conditions Cosby scourges, but also what the hip hop generation is contending with today—like destabilized black families, the flight of work leaving a dead-end trail of joblessness in our inner-cities, record incarcerations, and the devastating collapse of once thriving neighborhoods. Finally, Bell openly acknowledges structural complicity in maintaining the racial status quo, missed in much of Cosby's critique of the black poor. To his credit, Bell is careful to sidestep that camp of naysayers who "assert with equal vehemence that blaming failure on racism is an excuse; that we need to get up off our dead asses, drop the welfare tit, stop having 'illegitimate' babies, and find jobs like everybody else."[266] From all that Bell has said, what is quite evident is that there is a need for a balanced community's conversation about the state of the black poor, with a frank review of the historic and institutional factors and their role, rather than an all-out witch-hunt of those who are the most vulnerable and least able to defend themselves against powerful figures like a Cosby, and who become grist for the neoconservative blame mill.

"Lifting As I Climb"

Most that are interested in the Cosby's debate can surely agree that where the blame lies can be settled another day. For now, there is little to argue about the devastation terrorizing our faltering community. Quite frankly, it is under siege—in the midst of another dangerous Middle Passage on dry land. The great tragedy of the hour is that arguably we, as a people, have not fully realized what's at stake, nor taken the necessary but difficult steps to salvage future generations. While Cosby's diatribe may have been meant for black youth, even the black poor, in actuality, I take it as an indictment upon us all. Their present plight does not affect them alone. The condition of black youth is a moral barometer of the overall health of the black community. It is a reality check to the state of black America, and unfortunately, it tells us what we already know: we're in crisis mode. In many ways, seemingly our community is less well off than pre-sixties days; Cosby's public pulpit didn't have to tell us that. Our desolate neighborhoods, our teen relatives in prison, the plague of joblessness already told the story of our teeming frustration and disillusionment. "It takes a village" hasn't helped much. That trusted baton of community interdependence—"Remember where you come from. Don't forget your people"—has somehow slipped from the grasp of the present elder generation. What has happened, departing from that historical precedence of "lifting as I climb,"[267] the black community has equivocated perilously, to the point of apathy, in its moral duty to this hip hop generation. The pitiful truth of the matter is that that historic sense of mission, "lifting as I climb," parlayed today as "giving back"—which was once a respectable social virtue of the nineteenth- and mid-twentieth centuries that anchored the black middle-class's moral responsibility to its less well-off brothers and sisters—has drifted in the twenty-first century. Something went sinisterly awry. That very generation that Cosby disparages uncompromisingly throughout this nation had had this to say about themselves, the baby-boomer generation and their Cosby elders. One popular manchild of the hip-hop generation, Bakari Kitwana, in his forceful text, *The Hip Hop Generation: Young Blacks and The Crisis in African-American Culture*, bitterly accuses the black leadership of apathy bordering on moral negligence: "For hip hop generationers, it is difficult to find instances where Black baby boomers in mainstream leadership are collectively making a difference in the lives of young Blacks who constitute a significant portion of Black America."[268] What could explain this gross moral neglect? parents being berated by the children. Coming from two different perspectives seemingly, yet Cosby and Kitwana share different sides of the same coin about the moral dereliction of parents and of the black leadership.

Regrettably, at a time when it is ever more urgent to establish much needed buffers for threatened manchildren, the commitment to "lift as we climb" has fallen on hard times like so many other communal values nurtured by racial struggle and segregated outsider status. Its noble mission has been waysided by that rugged, middle-and upper-class individualism—much of it tied to affirmative action opportunities—though mums the word—"I did it by my own hands," in essence, "by my own bootstraps," and so should you is how it's scornfully tossed out to needy youth, who desperately desire a helping hand to mentor them into their success.

"Has the Black Middle-Class Lost Its Mind?"

Although his views are being hotly debated around the country, Cosby might just be on to something worth rethinking. Whether it amounts to the black middle-class losing its mind, I cannot vouch for that. For even as I belabor the strident role of institutional racism in creating conditions of black social death and demise throughout this book, black responsibility must not be shuffled to the wayside in any earnest haste to implicate only external factors for the distressing quality of our children's lives, the endless despair that accompanies their sojourn into young adulthood, and that of our unsecured families. There is a personal accountability expected of every citizen who shares a common constitutional communion. It was never a question for our foreparents. One of the triumphs of black history is that in spite of the horrendous lynching and legal resistance to our foreparents' progress, with less they did more in order to give each generation a fighting chance. While actor and director Denzel Washington was promoting his film, *The Great Debaters*, he had this criticism for parents.

> Our children's problems are our fault—we created and allowed this environment for them. He remains convinced that it still takes a village. But despite all the negative press about our kids, a lot of great work is getting done, and this film is a call to teachers and community leaders to keep fighting.[269]

In all fairness to Cosby, his remedy is not to abandon the black community to its own disadvantaged devices, but to go there and make a difference. "We have to go in there—forget about telling your child to go into the Peace Corps—it is right around the corner. They are standing on the corner and they can't speak English."[270] One of his recent contributions is the joint book project with psychiatrist Alvin Poussaint, *Come On People*, a down-to-earth sort of guide with steps and stories to personal empowerment. Journalist Juan Williams credits Cosby's remarks of self-help as "just plain old common sense." No, in Williams' opinion, the black middle-class has not lost its mind. For him, if the black poor are ever to overcome the vices of poverty, then they must make "tough choices" for deferred gratification. As opposed to buying brand-name sneakers, educating their children must be the "top priority."[271] "Nobody is going to save them, but themselves," is his final word of wisdom. Let us be honest. The more conservative among us make a convincing case. Our children are lagging behind academically, not because they lack the intellectual capacity but because, in many instances, superficial labels bought into are undermining their success like "selling out" and of "trying to be white." Did we forget to teach them that standards of excellence have never been the privileged domain of only one community? Across race and class lines African Americans strove for literacy—stolen it when they had to—and faced bloody mobs to access educational opportunities. *Brown* fought a hard fight to break open the front doors of opportunity to black children's hope. Even more, no middle-class African American has achieved anything without hard work in school. Success was never given; it was hard-earned. Few of us can boast of coming from privileged backgrounds. But many more came from hardworking homes. "Take command of English grammar." Cosby was right there.[272] It's been essential to Dyson's success. Look at how he uses words as strategic ammunition in his ideological skirmishes. How far can any professional really hope to climb, not just black, in accessing mainstream opportunities without some facility with the English language? Job-readiness skills likewise are required for our youth. As teens, they need opportunities to develop these all important marketable skills for trade in the marketplace, not just when they mature into adults. Some already have families for whom they provide support and financial help. As one neoconservative espouses, such life skills will remove black children beyond the locality of their crime-infested surroundings to prepare them to be competitive in a technocratic job marketplace.[273]

Besides, manchildren are not competing in a sixties' world but a global marketplace with stiffer competition, which neither cares nor knows about the historic black freedom struggle, and where competitive spaces are being fought for viciously. On the road to their success, participating in positive peer role modeling, in Boys and Girls Clubs, in political arts movements, in rites-of-passage programs, mentoring programs, youth groups in churches, anywhere there are positive examples of excellence and achievement are necessary if they are to be rescued. With only one life to live, manchildren must fight to win.

In the end, although certain sectors of the black community and its leadership have been quite ambivalent, to the point of being apathetic, about what is happening to young black people—and yes, Cosby embodies that black ambivalence. Yet, he's honest. But just the same, black upper middle-class and middle-class people can ill-afford the luxury of distancing ourselves from the struggle of poor blacks and their children. Being true to the spirit of our noble history, their struggle is the struggle of all black people. This solidarity is the greatest moral currency black people possess in a global frontier century.

CHAPTER 10:

What Has the Church Done for Black Youth Lately?
A Uth Turn Model*

Had I met people like you while I was out, it would have made the difference.
Valedictorian of the NYTS's Sing Sing Degree Program

I want to prevent at-risk youth from making the same mistakes I did.
Outreach Coordinator Lance Cruell, Uth Turn

Our major goal is to close the door on recidivism and to help our young people transition back into their communities.
Rev. C. Vernon Mason, Chief Executive Officer

"Had I met people like you while I was out, it would have made the difference," are solemn words of praise and gratitude coming from a graduate of the New York Theological Seminary's Sing Sing Degree Program, and now a Uth Turn counselor. Such a heartfelt tribute alludes to what faith-and community-based models of treatment can do like Uth Turn. Using the broad experiences and talents of the formerly incarcerated to make a difference in the lives of young people, in conflict with the criminal justice system, is what Uth Turn does. The brainchild of the Reverend Dr. Calvin Butts of Abyssinian Baptist Church, New York City and the Reverend Dr. William Howard, then the president of New York Theological Seminary, and now the pastor of Bethany Baptist Church in Newark, New Jersey, Uth Turn was started in February 1999. Since then, more than 3,000 young people have matriculated through the halls of the program. Conceived as a faith-based intervention program, Uth Turn provides community-focused life-skills training, mentoring, educational and vocational preparation, crisis management, and community services to vulnerable youth ages 13 to 21.

A former civil rights attorney, Reverend C. Vernon Mason[274] currently serves as Chief Executive Officer for the Uth Turn initiative. From its inception, he has led Uth Turn into an unparalleled success with some of the hard to reach black and Hispanic youth.[275] Unequivocal about its mission as a change agent, Uth Turn advocates creating a society with less crime delinquency and substance abuse while assisting those at-risk youth to make positive changes and successfully transition into adulthood. "I think some of our success can also be attributed to the fact that these young people, many of them marginalized and tossed aside, are given another chance, and from this they begin to see they have a future. We give them an opportunity to empower themselves, to take charge of their lives," is how Rev. Mason proudly credits its phenomenal success. Currently, being observed as a national model, Uth Turn combines the best of the community, schools and organizations of faith.

Philosophy and Mission of Uth Turn

The philosophy of Uth Turn is premised upon two anchors that have been critical in the survival of people of African descent: faith and education. A protégée of Dr. Benjamin Mays, President of Morehouse College during the years of Mason's matriculation, he was significantly influenced by Mays's commitment to race progress and human uplift. Backdropped against that prestigious past, Mason has taken those very same core values that were instilled in him as a young man, and infuses them into the Uth Turn initiative. The pivot role of faith and education in grounding the success of the program will become evident as the Uth Turn story is told. To those at-risk young people, Uth Turn shines as a beacon of hope, liberation, freedom, advancement, and progress. It represents a commitment to reintegrating troubled youth back into the community as contributing members.

Doing a remarkable job in redirecting the lives of at-risk young people, Uth Turn, first of all, is located at 12 church centers where it receives some of its referrals. Young people at-risk arrive at the program in a variety ways: from the court, family members, or by word of mouth. The program is currently operating in 12 New York City neighborhoods. On September 7, 2004, Uth Turn launched Bethany Uth Turn,[276] its first national site in Newark, New Jersey. This was a collaboration with Bethany Baptist Church, Essex Residential Community Home and the New Jersey Juvenile Commission, an initiative allowing Uth Turn to replicate its youth development model on a national scale.

What is Unique About the Program?

One of the unique aspects of the program is how it uses people (staff) who have been "through the fire," who have been at-risk, and even imprisoned. The Uth Turn model has formerly incarcerated working with at-risk youth. In its model, facilitators come with a special kind of first-hand knowledge utilized to benefit the recovery of at-risk youth; for young people do not feel that they are talking to an out-of-touch authority figure. The youth in the program know that many of the teachers and facilitators in charge have been "at- risk" once in their own life or even imprisoned.

When a young person turns to Uth Turn, he or she is introduced to something radically different than many of the recovery programs out there. First, the outstanding teachers and facilitators, hand-picked to work in the program, tend to be, not always, graduates of the New York Theological Seminary's Master of Professional Studies (MPS) degree program at Sing Sing Prison. Outreach coordinator Lance Cruell, who spent three and half years at Sing Sing, stresses the uniqueness of Uth Turn.

Since I come from where many of those in the program come from, I can relate to them and show them how to turn their lives around like I did. I meet with them three times a week, sometimes even going to their homes to help them improve their grades and show them how to get out of gangs, if they are faced with that problem. One of the real antidotes to curbing young boys who drift into crime and violence is the presence of a father, so I'm working on bringing them back together.

Uth Turn is one of the few, if not the only, programs in this nation that can draw from a pool of professionals who have had life experiences that can immediately serve the treatment needs of young people: who are street youth, gang members, young people with pending or prior conflicts with the law. Better said by Mason, "We are the only youth program in the nation using this proven and effective resource. NYTS graduates are real-life role models who have faced many of the same challenges and pitfalls as these young people and have learned to conquer them. They are lifelines who help rescue these youth from criminality, drug use and despair." Graduates from the Seminary's MPS program serve as facilitators, mentors, and youth advocates. Besides being intelligent and gifted, facilitators possess that rare quality of having a passion for turning young lives around.

Seminarians involved in urban ministries studies also contribute their knowledge and skill-based to the success of the Uth Turn model. With its association with the New York Theological Seminary, for those familiar with the emergence of urban ministry, Uth Turn has created a new paradigm for urban youth ministry, cutting-edge and unique.

Most importantly, the possibility of introducing this model to other penal systems would be a huge step in the right direction toward rehabilitation rather than a lopsided emphasis on punishment. With the MPS degree as part of the empowerment equation, education has made the difference in the lives of the formerly incarcerated, and so will it in the lives of those at-risk youth. Correctional facilitates around the nation could benefit from what Uth Turn is doing. Graduates whose lives are turned around come back to the community to help at-risk youth. The objective is to embrace all in the village circle and not escalate a vicious social cycle. Facilitators are involved in meaningful work, and it makes all the difference. Both facilitators and recovering youth benefit from low recidivism rates.

A Partner—The Role of the Church

All 12 operational sites in New York City are housed in churches. These institutions of faith provide office and youth development space, administrative support as well as mentors. Because churches help anchor the neighborhood and community, they become most effective safe havens for youth; mentors are also there. It is really a "no brainer." According to Mason, this arrangement really inspires church members to be mentors for these at-risk youth. Their initial arm's length reservation was turned into embracing the community's children. At the church site, mentors can guide youth in their education and career aspirations beyond the time they spend in the Uth Turn Program. This point is critical. Because the Uth Turn program does not encourage dependent relationships after being released from the program, having young people anchored in a church context increases connectedness—a sense of belonging and communal accountability. At the nexus of the church, faith and education are intertwined for the purpose of engendering successful, productive members of society.

The active role of congregations in outreach to youth represents a paradigm shift in many cases. While the church has prayed for the formerly incarcerated or even had prison ministries, the role of operating as a site for youth rehabilitation is very different. The Uth Turn model has presented itself as one way in which the local congregation can become communally involved with the formerly incarcerated and its at-risk youth. Mason explains, "Formerly, churches prayed for persons in prison but didn't work with them or accept them as members. More churches are recognizing the need to work with re-entry programs, to contribute in supporting the formerly incarcerated."

Before Uth Turn made inroads into churches, there was still a lot of fear in the church community about working with the formerly incarcerated. For instance, in 1999, the board of one church opposed plans of being used as one of the Uth Turn sites because of fears of the formerly incarcerated and at-risk youth. The pastor took the program initiative to the congregation over the objections of the board. He discussed the program and its objectives, and he took a hand-raising poll: "Who in the congregation had," according to Mason, "or had a relative or friend among the formerly incarcerated?" The response of the congregation was overwhelming by the numbers who raised their hand. Most had a relative, friend, or someone incarcerated or formerly incarcerated. No one had been talking about it, maybe because of shame, but experiencing it nonetheless. This experience educated the board about what they didn't want in the church but was already there. "That very church continues to work with us even today," Mason commented. "That was a good lesson for the church."

Curriculum Model

Even more impressive, in 2006, Uth Turn worked with 581 court-adjudicated youths (from the ages of 13-21) and 92 percent of them had no further problems with the criminal justice system. In the words of Mason, "To translate that roughly in dollars and cents is that the state pays $100,000 a year to incarcerate a youth, whereas it costs Uth Turn only $2,000 per individual." These figures alone suggest, in his opinion, that it makes far more sense to invest in prevention, which will produce the added benefit of keeping young people in the community.

When youth are referred to Uth Turn, they receive a comprehensive assessment to address specific needs of each client. Along with an individually designed course of treatment, they all benefit from individual and group counseling, stress management and conflict resolution programs, education and employment assistance, as well as social service referrals and support to combat substance abuse. By providing a supportive, nurturing environment, Uth Turn helps young people develop interpersonal problem solving, ethical and cognitive skills that will lead them toward their success.

Before leaving the Uth Turn program, at-risk young people must matriculate through the core values curriculum. It is divided into seven modules:

A. Positive self-image
B. Internal Locus of Control
C. Future Orientation (not instant gratification or living for today)
D. Coping Skill
E. Conflict Resolutions
F. Positive Peer Interaction and Relationship Skill
G. Community Responsibility

Concentrating in these areas is to improve the following areas of personal development among youth: personal mastery, social acceptance, school performance, parental trust, self-esteem and employability.

The Role of Community Responsibility

Of particular interest was the role of community responsibility and reduction of youth recidivism. Mason contends that feeling a sense of community responsibility on the part of youth is especially important to reducing social isolationism. Raising their level of connectedness to themselves, their families and external environment grounds their sense of being a part of a community. In other words, possessing that feeling of being somebody—"You are somebody"—could make a difference between recovery and recidivism. Thus, their involvement in the community assures them that they are more than a resident. The community belongs to them as contributing members; it is their village. The underlying assumption is that if youth feel that they are a part of a community, that it belongs to them; then they are less likely to prey upon that community. Their relationship is not parasitic but they are partners in its prosperity. Uth Turn helps them to see the community differently and their role in it.

One way that Uth Turn achieves this shift in mindset is by promoting leadership through community service activities. One of the most notable community outreach projects of Uth Turn was "Miracle on 138th Street – Feeding 5000." Uth Turn partnered with the National Basketball Players Association, Feed the Children and the Abyssinian Baptist Church to distribute food to 5,000 families in Harlem in 2003. From a set of organized experiences such as that, youth make that community connection.

Conclusion

Uth Turn could not do this alone. Without their collaborative partners who have a visible stake in youth empowerment, the program would be waging a formidable uphill battle. Significant partners are: the United Way, the New York State Office of Children and Family Services, the New York Juvenile Justice Commission, and the Taproot Foundation. This unique collaboration of social service agencies, the criminal justice system, schools, community groups, faith-based organizations and ex-offenders strives to deter young people from a life of delinquency and incarceration to invest in themselves and their community.

CHAPTER 11

Where the Eagles Fly*
The Success of Eagle Academy for Young Men

The new Eagle Academy is a tremendous addition to the district and will inspire future generations to soar as high, if not, higher than an eagle.

Assemblyman Michael Benjamin of New York

The No. 1 lesson we've learned through all this is that if we want to sustain a level of success for young men, we have to start earlier than high school.

David Banks, Principal of Eagle Academy

"Being a senior is being a part of a must needed change in society for black males to succeed."

Marcus Thompson, Senior at Eagle Academy

Introduction to Eagle Academy

As David Banks, the founding Academy principal, slowly stood up to the mike, the boys quieted down for the day's schedule. In the cafeteria, which readily converts into a morning townhall, with a sniff of fresh bacon still scenting the energy-filled air, is where the school activities are outlined, comments made, and accolades handed out to young achievers before the beaming stares of their peers. As I looked on, the boys were reminded to bring back their permission slip for the upcoming visit to Fox Studios in New Jersey. Although little known or publicized, media mogul Rupert Murdoch is one of those patron saints dedicated to these aspiring young men in the South Bronx. But more importantly, their upcoming trip highlights the public and private investment necessary in guaranteeing the success of creative educational initiatives like Eagle Academy. In the twenty-first century, as this new frontier of public education is being remapped, joint ventures such as this one attest overwhelmingly to the much-needed alliances in public education to halt the downward spiral that even a federal initiative like No Child Left Behind could not arrest. The bustling townhall ends with the young men shaking hands with a fresh entourage of visitors, who have pilgrimaged from far and near to the renowned Eagle's nest, better known as Eagle Academy, before they marched off to their waiting classrooms.

A Call to Action: The Mission of Eagle Academy

Eagle Academy was conceived with a lofty mission in mind: "inspire future generations to soar as high, if not, higher than an eagle." Spearheaded by One Hundred Black Men and David Banks, the present principal of Eagle Academy, it was to be no small achievement. High and lifted up, Eagle Academy is meant to be an institution that embodies the spirit and majesty in which young Black and Hispanic males can imagine themselves metaphorically as eagles, with the strength, courage, and vision to excel in an environment riddled with adverse challenges to their survival and success. At the Academy, the unequivocal mission is for the young men "to fly sky high." "We dubbed it the Eagle Academy because of the majesty of what an eagle represents," said President Philip Banks, Jr. of One Hundred Black Men, Inc. of New York President. "The eagle doesn't flock. It soars above the clouds." Conspicuously displayed here and there, an assortment of eagles adorns the school setting to remind the boys of their true destiny.

These young men understand how privileged they are to be in a school like Eagle Academy, and they seriously treasure the possibility of their "one chance" to succeed as a hard-won trophy. Hard work is a must on the part of these young men. They know from the hard-knocks they face in city streets on a daily basis that second chances are begrudged the meager station from which they sprung in life. They are not unfamiliar with the dire statistics anticipating their failure. In New York City, there is only a 30 percent graduation rate among black boys, and 24 percent graduation for black boys in the Bronx. At Eagle Academy, they are not alone in fighting those odds. Aside from the watchful eye of the committed staff helping them to battle those frightful odds, icons of black achievement dot the school's academic landscape, hailing them on. Indeed, the spirit of the African proverb, "I am because we are, we are because I am," comes alive at the Academy. In an academic environment where inspiration is a constant, around every corner, how can they not achieve?

To his credit, Principal Banks has saturated the school atmosphere with high expectations. "Excellence, both in character and scholarship, opens doors and provides a bridge to equality," is his concerted opinion. From his daily efforts, Banks proves that academic excellence does not alone belong within the privileged preserve of the wealthy, but that poor, young men in the South Bronx can value such noble achievements too.

In addition, Principal Banks unashamedly draws his own inspiration from his office-lined wall: a mounted newspaper clipping of his father and himself with the touching tribute— "the wind behind my wings"—an impressively framed magazine cover features Mayor Corey Booker, other artistic photographs and portraits of distinguished historical personalities like the Tuskegee Airmen, a Buffalo Soldier, Malcolm X, Muhammad Ali—high achievers are all of them. Awards upon awards acknowledge Banks' own contribution to excellence. Close at hand was a copy of Bill Coby's *Come on People* on eye-catching display.

Yes, the young men who matriculate at the Academy have noble aspirations for themselves. Already, they understand that they are being tapped as future leaders in and across society. Teambuilding and servicing the community are marked as core values that the Academy seeks to instill in these young fledglings. The Academy is not selfish in its aim, though. It understands that unless it takes the community along with them, it has failed in one of its most sacred trusts: to uplift the community as its young eaglets soar. "The Eagle Academy will make a difference, not only in our lives, but in our communities." Furthermore, the Academy is proud to link its mission to students', faculty's, and community's performance in academic excellence, ethical behavior, and personal responsibility. In general, this strategic partnership acknowledges that education does not happen in a vacuum. There must be partners. It must have self-interested stakeholders. The framers of the No Child Left Behind Act of 2001 could have learned a great deal from the on-the-ground Eagle Academy's model.

A Leader Who Dares to Care: Principal David Bank's Vision Statement

Inspired by the call to action at the historic 1995 Million Man March, Principal Banks came back to his community on a mission to turn the tide of the grim statistics decimating young black males in New York City. He wanted to be part of the solution and not fall into the hollow category of complaining about the problem. Here's what he is up against in his boys succeeding in a climate that has already counted out black youth: "A disproportionately high number of black men in the United States cycle in and out of the criminal justice system, and that a recent study found that nearly half of black men 16 to 64 in New York City were not working last year." Banks expresses strong feeling about Black and Latino boys feeding the upstate New York prison pipelines. He is convinced, "...The solution to the crisis of minority boys lies in education." Coming from an educator, Banks' sentiment is not surprising. His remark also reflects the deep faith of the black community in its long tradition of investing in education to escape the burdens of poverty.

More than rhetoric, Banks is right that the "Eagle Academy is a national story. The issues that are facing us in New York City are echoed throughout the nation. If we are able to effect positive change through mentoring and a commitment to building on the foundation of character, and we will, we will have started a revolution in the education of our youngsters." Banks' wisdom strongly reminisces that old bootstrap philosophy: "hard work, quality education, changing value systems, celebrating intellectual achievement and mentoring are of the utmost importance in the elevation of those at the bottom."[277]

To make hope concrete there, "The start of a new beginning," emblems the Academy wall. Thus, in spite of the odds, Banks is confident enough that Eagle Academy gives its young men a fighting chance. However, he has lost some. He is very frank about that, and shares a poignant letter from a young man in prison, who confesses to the error of his ways and wishes that he had listened to Banks more. He even requested that Banks would read the letter to the young men during the morning townhall. Although he might lose some, Banks is saving more. Besides, Banks is not so preoccupied with personal responsibility on the part of his young men to the exclusion of everything else. Their being given a chance, even a second chance, is just as important as their accepting responsibility for their bad choices or failure. In the end, his irrepressible optimism about the future is best captured in these redemptive words: "I'm beyond hopeful for the boys in this school," he confides. "To fail is not an option here." He goes on to declare that "Eagle Academy is an idea whose time has come and [it fills] a great need in the community."

Where the Eagles Soar: The Journey of Eagle Academy

The first of its kind in New York State, it is an all-boys public high school.[278] The school is the brainchild of a public-private joint venture between the New York City's Department of Education, One Hundred Black Men, a civic organization, that comes with the support of community heavy hitters like Percy Sutton, David Dinkin, Bill Cosby, and other key advocates.

The $41.5 million future site for the school will be located in the East Tremont section of the Bronx. Expected to open in 2009, the building will offer state-of-the-arts facilities for this ambitious venture into quality education, an investment at the ground level in at-risk young urban males to help them succeed. Eagle Academy's first and present home is in the Middle School 166 and the Bronx School for Law, Government and Justice in Morrisania. Currently in their shared facilities, space is tight, but the young men make due. More interested in achieving their destiny than being bothered with the smaller details of overcrowded classroom space, but the intimacy of it all reinforces their status of chosenness, of being part of a "grand experiment," as reiterated by Banks. Certainly, little inconveniences like lack of sufficient classroom space can't stand in the way of what Principal Banks envisions as the grand picture for his boys. As he looks through his office window upon the sprawling Eagle complex in the final stages of completion, Banks knows that in about a year from now, the fruition of their hard labor will take tangible shape in the Academy settling into their long-awaited nest.

Soon the Academy's own home site will boast essential academic amenities such as a science suite, an art room, a music room, a gymnasium and weight room, a suite of offices for guidance services, a library, and 14 classrooms. There are only 567 spaces for students selected.

Students must apply to get in Eagle Academy. Already, the popularity of the school is beyond their space's capacity to actually handle. So impressive, one academic year, there were 6,000 applicants for the limited 100 spaces at the school. One of the attractive features of the Academy is its smaller classes, a conducive learning environment with individual tutoring. Those who get in can't help but feel special, part of a great academic experiment. Parent Tawana Dunham writes: "I am really happy that my son was accepted into the Eagle Academy for young men. It is about time someone noticed our young men need help, guidance, and encouragement from positive male figures." With political will on the part of the Bloomberg administration, the advocacy role of key local politicians and activists, as well as the commitment of the One Hundred Black Men, Eagle Academy's existence witnesses to the fact that if there's a will, there's a way.

The school draws from its mostly minority neighborhood, Melrose, in the South Bronx. In 2005, when it first opened, 56.4 percent of Eagle Academy's students were black, 37.3 percent were Hispanic. Over half of these boys come from economic backgrounds that qualify them as eligible for free lunch.

Where Single-Sexed Schools Work

Without a great deal of fanfare attached, Principal Banks is engaged in the critical work of remaking the nature of public education for failing young urban males. One of his novel ideas is that a curriculum has to be devised based on how boys learn, an emphasis on hands-on experiences, and attending to boys' natural competitive nature. Rather than cater to top-down standards at the expense of practical classroom experiences and from real interaction with students, the curriculum at Eagle Academy boasts a critical relevance to the young males it serves, and possesses a real potential to be transformative and radical with it prioritizing the needs of its student population first. The context that presented itself as most conducive to that style of learning was an all-boys school.

Without apology, Banks is an unabashed disciple of single-gender schools,[279] and firmly believes, in the case of Eagle Academy, that it will address the academic disparity of Black and Latino communities. Public education with its present challenges has been found wanting when it comes to educating young urban males, in his opinion. Taken from someone who knows well the dismal statistics of the failing public education system in holding and graduating black youth with a solid academic foundation, other viable alternatives had to be explored for Black and Hispanic boys. To do less was to underserve the academic needs of "No Child Left Behind" youth. Herein enters single-sex schools. Banks had no illusion about what he was up against: "There is a crisis of inner city young men who are not making it to the finish line. If that's not a crisis, I don't know what is. At every level, African-American and Latino boys are doing far worse than every other group. Eagle Academy is a full-fledged response to this crisis." In taking this long-shot, Principal Banks is honest enough to admit his fears, "Far too many [African American and Hispanic] young men are not making it. Single-sex education may not be the answer but it is worth the try." But Eagle Academy benefits from the wisdom of African-American child and adolescent psychiatrist Michael Pratt, "Black boys need Black men to be consistently and personally involved with them for this to happen." Pratt continues in this vein, "Social and moral responsibility comes from self-esteem. Self-esteem stems from pride. Modeling behavior is desperately needed by young African-American males to identify and internalize racial pride and self-confidence." His counsel promotes the single-gender education alternative for young African American males. And Banks is unafraid to try something innovative to save his boys. His enthusiasm about an idea— whose time has come—is only exceeded by the expectation of strong results of closing the minority achievement gap.

Angelo Ruiz gives a student's perspective on single-sex education:

> Most boys at the school don't like the idea of a single-sex school when they first arrive; often, their parents chose the school for them. But once they get into the rhythm of the school, they grow to like its student-centered approach, all-boys environment and even its strict discipline.

Angelo concedes, "Not having girls in class makes us be more focused."

One-on-One Mentoring: One Hundred Black Men, Inc.

One of the most attractive and strongest components of the program is the one-on-one mentoring. Parents, mostly female-headed households, are looking for that male mentoring influence in the lives of their boys. Putting action to their talk, One Hundred Black Men is fulfilling that role. On the frontlines with their charges, they are keeping their part of the bargain. They are executing that sacred trust invested in them. Students are matched up based on their career interests and/or social needs, with a member of One Hundred Black Men for the duration of high school. Getting men to stand up to address the ills of our community, to be counted, is what the One Hundred Black Men's mentoring presence represents.

"One of the most reliable predictors of whether a boy will succeed or fail in high school rests on a single question: does he have a man in his life to look up to?"[280] At Eagle Academy, for many of the boys who have never known their fathers or had consistent positive male presence in their lives, this mentoring program promises a tremendous difference in turning the odds around in favor of these young Black and Hispanic males. "Many of his students," according to Banks, "are being raised by their mothers and grandmothers, a common problem in neighborhoods like the South Bronx. Before coming to Eagle Academy, many of the boys had no male role models to look up to outside of their school." Banks is right. Black mothers are anxious about help to raise their sons into productive young men. At the Academy, the role of the mentor is key to keeping the young men on task. Not in just the big career or major life issues will one find his vigilant presence. It could be something as basic as addressing a minor behavior problem. "The school, for instance, informs the mentor, and he, in turn, speaks to the student about it on the phone or in person during the Saturday academy." Unabashedly, Banks confesses, "We play the role of big brothers and dads." To that extent, the school "organizes a 'mentor appreciation' event for Father's Day." Student Joshua Mozon, 17, said, "He looks up to his mentor, a leader at the city's Metropolitan Transit Authority. He helps me with problems, with issues at home, anything. I go to my parents and then I go to him." In truth, Eagle Academy represents a strategic partnership among a host of stakeholders: its students, principals, administrators, teachers, parents, mentors, and community supporters.

Passing on the mentoring ethic and tradition at Eagle Academy is important. There is a mentoring role for the young men themselves to play. As Eagle Scholars adhering to the Principles of the Leadership program, they have to peer-mentor one another and represent an "agent of change in their community."

The Role of Discipline

Following the rules at Eagle Academy is quite important. Discipline ranks as a high priority, what Banks calls "tough love." The Academy is aware of the fact that many of their students come with serious disciplinary challenges, but that's not perceived as a deterrent to the staff. They are committed to turning these young boys' lives around. Adding order to a boy's life in disarray is critical to academic success: "Boys come to us already off-track, but there are enough men here to provide the discipline they crave," volunteers Principal Banks. From my visit to Eagle Academy, I can attest to the strong presence of male teachers in the classroom and male staff surrounding the boys to give them firm guidance.

Banks is convinced along with its founding partner, One Hundred Black Men, that for their "at-risk population of poor, urban, minority boys, many from single-mother households, [it is important for the Academy to] give them strong doses of exactly the kind of school environment they need." So Eagle Academy has a disciplined, academically rigorous, and culturally relevant environment to get results. Excuses are not abided easily. Banks believes that orchestrating this kind of intentional environment is a form of critical intervention into the lives of these young men to save them from violence and the hopelessness of gangs, or even worse. On target in his thoughtful analysis, "They're big, they're angry, and they can't read. And that's a recipe for an explosion," Banks laments.

Beyond the classrooms and halls of the school, this positive behavior carries over into the home life of these students. The boys agree, "Our behavior at home starts to improve after a while. We won't talk back to our parents as much. We won't do things to get attention. Ever since I came here, I've calmed down, I've matured more."

A College Bound Curriculum

The school is determined to keep students on track to college. The ninth grade is not too soon to identify career aspirations. During a class visit, I spoke to Eddie Rodriguez and Darkari Mayo, both ninth graders. Mayo had already completed his admission essay for Tusk University. He allowed me a glance; medicine is his interest. Rodriguez is drawn to forensics science; not just decaying corpses, he wants to excavate crime scenes. In a government class visited, Korey Malcolm, at all of fifteen, assured me that little kids could look up to President Barack Obama. An important goal of Eagle Academy is to create an intimate learning environment that deters low dropout rates and increases student performance.

To achieve such astounding results is not easy. Longer school days are routine. They last until 5:30 p.m. After regular classes end, study groups and homework help are part of the routine menu. Time on task is seen as a gateway to academic success. Saturday sessions, from 9 a.m. to noon, conclude the school week. The curriculum also includes sports. Although the mission of Eagle Academy is not sports-centered, for rambunctious boys having an intramural outlet is just as important as studying to healthy youth development. Their after-school activities accomplish a dual purpose: they involve the boys in tutorial activities and engage them in constructive pursuits to keep them off the streets in the afternoons and evenings on the weekends.[281]

Conclusion

Perhaps, Principal Banks' greatest contribution to the success of Eagle Academy is his ability, if not humility, to roll up his sleeve and get down and dirty in the nuts and bolts of running an all-boys institution. With equal fervor, he and his staff are deeply invested in the lives of these young men. A combination of these qualities has produced what I call the "Banks factor": his ability to inspire loyalty in his staff, create teams that are effective educators, nurture a whole-hearted commitment to the charge in their safe-keeping, maintain a quality curriculum, and yet hold the vision steady—may very well be the recipe for his unparalleled success.

His dynamic, personable and non-stop vigilance guarantees the standards at Eagle. Banks' ability to maintain the hands-on quality of engagement as he shifts roles to his new charge as superintendent of the growing numbers of Eagle Academies being designed for the New York City's public school system, begs the question. He has been given the portfolio to oversee replicating 14 other Eagle Academies in failing school districts in New York City. Can Banks maintain the momentum in providing a quality education and educational experience desperately needed by urban boys without the "Banks factor" in the day-to-day operations of an Eagle Academy? Can he maintain that "special something" that attracts his followers, the young men, to be at the Academy past school hours? learning and basking in an environment where they know that they are among the elect in the Black and Hispanic communities.

Finally, young men's hopes are pasted all over the Eagle's nest. It was a sobering as well as a humbling experience to enter the sanctum where care is tangible and hope alive in shaping the lives of these much-beloved minority males. And the young men know it—that they are loved. When Banks meets them in the hall, he knows their names, where they are headed academically, and what each eaglet's particular success story is. It would seem rather difficult for one person to keep up with so many youth. But like a proud father, each child is valued and respected in his own right. Principal Banks might be what the boys call him, but Father Banks is how they feel about him. And I'm sure the feeling is mutual. They are Banks' chosen. I confess that I'm a convert of what Banks is doing at Eagle Academy in the South Bronx, and it reinforces tangible hope for the struggle of manchildren all over our nation.

CHAPTER 12

An Unsigned Letter: Black Mothering in the Trenches

I am an African-American mother of a young African American male. I have a story to tell.

On August 29, 1994, my husband and I had an appointment with a foster care agency so we could adopt a child. As part of that interview we were required by law to look through what is called the *Blue Book*. The *Blue Book* is a book of picture after picture of children available for adoption. Almost all those children were African American.

That same day I began keeping a journal for the child that would be mine. This is what I wrote about the *Blue Book* children: "It made me sort of sad to see so many children available for adoption. They represent a lot of love." Love was what I had on my mind. I was looking for a child to love.

By August 3, 1995, I found my child. The agency had showed us a five-year old boy we agreed we wanted. Because he was in foster care at the time, first, we had to become his foster parents so we could later adopt him. Becoming a foster mother meant I would be joining my child in one of the many "threatening conditions"[282] about which Dr. Cuffee speaks throughout her book.

Foster care is one of the "threatening conditions" our children face. Foster care is money driven: the "sicker" the children, the more money the state pays for their care.

I began to understand that my child (along with many others) was being labeled as dysfunctional by well-meaning people, and these labels were defining his life. To me he was "active." To his social worker, he was "hyperactive." To me he was "curious." To her he was "disruptive." This labeling was substantiating the foster-care money-value of my child. I met other foster parents who had entered the system primarily, if not totally, for the money-value of a foster child. As surely as a prison inmate is "money" in the prison system, my son was "money" in the foster care system.

Another "threatening condition" in my son's life was the public school system and its relationship with the counseling establishment. From at least first grade this "hyperactive anxious" child was in counseling and special education. As new labels began to emerge, he was described as "aggressive and depressed."

Soon he began to *become* his labels. By the time he was in his mid-teens, he was accurately described as very depressed. His personality traits included low self-esteem, a dearth of gratifying relationships, poor judgment under stress, and a compromised capacity for reality testing.

(I should note here that this African American male is definitely not a child whom his mother would expect could be safe in an encounter with a police officer —another threatening condition for any African American male. I have had to worry constantly that one day, when my son was not at home, I would answer the door to find a police officer standing there. And our family is a middle-class, middle income, church-going family. But, in reality, those advantages have meant little or nothing for my son.)

At the age of 16 he was not attending school anymore. He was awake all night and sleeping all day. He had become morbidly obese (another threatening condition) and a physical threat to me. He constantly lied, became secretive, and owned things I could not account for. I couldn't trust him, I became afraid of him and no matter how much I still loved him, I couldn't seem to help him. I only knew that his life was being paralyzed.

I later found out he was a member of a street gang (another threatening condition) and was participating in a lot of dangerous, life-threatening behavior. And yes, he had a gun "hold-up" in my house. It became obvious to me that, if he were pulled over by the police, he would end up dead or in jail. It was also obvious that if he were *not* pulled over by the police, he would still end up dead or in jail.

I have come to understand that as a young black man, he will have to live with "threatening conditions" the rest of his life. I also have come to understand that, as a young black man he does not have to be the *victim* of "threatening conditions." Today he knows that too. As I write this, he is a senior in a boarding school for at-risk teens. He is applying to colleges and has even identified a major he wants to pursue. He has a chance at life that he did not have two years ago. His mind and soul are more and more peaceful and at rest. And we are living one day at a time.

Now! Here is where I want to sit down with you and look you in the face. This is what I want to say to you: Never give up on our children. Never. With God, all things are possible. As a black mother, I have found strength I didn't know I had. I ended up kidnapping my son off the streets and out of the hands of criminals and street life. He was trapped. I thought I was trapped with him. I felt hopeless and helpless. But I tell you, with God, all things are possible.

Whoever you understand God to be and whatever name you use for God, the image that our Creator imprinted upon us and our children is indelible. Wherever your child and my child are today, we are a major part of their solution. Find a way! Never give up! We and our children are worth it.

Signed,
A Black Mother

EPILOGUE

"And I've looked over, and I've seen the promised land. I may not get there with you, but I want you to know tonight that we as a people will get to the promised land. So I'm happy tonight. I'm not worried about anything. I'm not fearing any man."

Martin Luther King Jr., Speech in Memphis, April 3, 1968, the day before King was assassinated

"The ultimate measure of a man is not where he stands in moments of comfort and convenience, but where he stands at times of challenge and controversy."
Martin Luther King Jr., *Strength to Love,* 1963

Trapped in a world of criminal justice bias, in a community mired in urban blight, a hostage to the misery of poverty and pain, when death by gunshot blast seems inevitable, in a high risk neighborhood is where he sleeps, rampant criminalization guarantees him the quickest passport to lockdown, arguably shut out of America's technocratic future, the black manchild haunts ghetto city-streets on borrowed time. Against that daily march of black death, made habitual for countless number of manchildren, is where they struggle with every breath they take for their very soul survival, their basic human right to life itself, no matter how hellish their urban trials.

From the grim commentary above, already we know that before manchildren can triumph out of life's starting blocks, their lives are already defaulted in a world that associates blackness with deficiencies. Ghettos that house these children's souls and bodies were not created by them. They live lives fated by conditions usually beyond their own tenuous choices, and as charged throughout this reader, maintained and perpetuated by unjust and racist institutional mechanisms that care less about the misery of black youth, and are sure to doom them to incarceration or premature death. Economic conditions are no better. Manchildren suffer further marginalization in the domestic economy with America's institutionalization of spare workers in an intensely competitive job market among unskilled laborers, with many employers preferring the "benefit-free" undocumented workers. Our youth face the grim shortage of communal resources to intervene propitiously in their situation, along with seeming parental inability or simply apathy about averting this tsunami of black demise and death.

What's more, the prison industrial complex personifies that this nation is divided and hostile, and that its growth is predicated upon an insatiable thirst for the destinies of African American youth. From the cradle, far too many casually resign themselves to the certainty of ending up in jail or prison someday. Confessed as, "it's part of life," prisons serve as the new college for black males. Some declare them the new high school. Social death and disposability await their stolen lives. They inherit this as their lost birthright, the crumbling legacy of the long overdue American dream. Past due is the national conversation about the criminal justice system and how it handles matters of prevention, interdiction, rehabilitation and inmates' re-entry into the community. As long as the black community is apathetic about this breaking crisis on our very doorsteps, countless number of manchildren will fall through the gaping breaches in our unreliable social safety net, which, of course, has never been secure for African American youth, and their human capital lost to the black community in disastrous proportions.

In writing this book, without mistakenly romancing manchildren's hard-earned lives, my task was to give voice to their life struggle and to express love and care as any surrogate parent would. Some might accuse me of indulging in all rhetoric and passion. And I plead guilty unashamedly by offering this refrain, defensively, perhaps, in the eyes of my accusers: dying is infinitely passionate. Indeed, manchildren often operates in an underworld that takes no prisoners. As raw shrieks of black death, spat out from their stumbling bodies, forsaken to the comfort of a cold-hearted pavement, their dying sticks in my mind as an unforgivable and unforgettable metaphor for black boys' lives. Their unmerciless deaths should strike at the heart of any caring humanity to resist disconnection to their tragic demise, to mourn their inhuman executions—every human being deserves better—to grieve their unrequited lives. Manchildren live no easy lives; nor do they die painless deaths. They die with unfinished dreams. That forsaken memory of their cut-short existences is invoked to advocate against every manchild's untimely demise. It attests to the abysmal frailness of young black male existence. This reader is indeed meant to breathe fresh hope into their helplessness and bound up their bleeding hearts. Many want to be saved. This fact encourages me to refuse any apology for the passion that infuses this project. I lay no claim to being an indifferent, apathetic academic to the murder of children.

I admit, also, that I am a soul writer whose passion for the souls of our nation's truly disinherited is insatiable. Thus, I cannot stand idly by while a nation treats children as beggars and sponsors conditions of death that irresponsibly trample on society's most vulnerable. Our country embraces a crippling myopia when it comes to manchildren, which is manifested in how public policy complicity is complicit in breeding conditions of poverty, violence and premature death, if not mandatory incarceration, for young black males. I also confess that I wrote these essays in such a manner that America would stop averting her eyes from the ugly realities afflicting black youth; that they might indeed trigger a crisis of conscience to produce timely intervention, not a nation's retreat into more moral legalism and victim-blaming indifference. Unapologetically, my task was to bare the vulnerable soul of the young black male, to handle the broken places in his life with infinite care, and finally to participate in a fiery brand of Sojourner Truth's truth-telling that would move the hearts of readers beyond moral apathy about the plight of young black males to become a healing hand in their redemption, to establish a radical presence of solidarity with those whom society has refused to salvage. Indeed, my moral outrage is borrowed from a like tradition of long ago, when slave mothers refused to be silenced when their children, their young black future, were placed on auction blocks as the fatal sign and symbol of devastation and annihilation to the sprouting of any secret seeds of freedom's hope.

Epilogue

On my moral watch, let it not be said I succumbed to an unfeeling apathy that did not save or spare the lives of children, of black youth, and a race's stolen young adulthood. I am inextricably involved here. These children are my future, too. And I am frightened enough about their future to do something. They must know that they are not alone. For me not to raise my voice, at this critical time in their history, in unison with caring people throughout this country, would be a grave dereliction of duty and to renege on my moral watch. The moral imperative is upon us. What we do can alter the fate of at least of one of these beleaguered manchildren; the one to whom we have been called to make a difference, whose destiny is inextricably bound up with our very own—a human debt owed to one another for occupying the planet as a community. Any forfeiture of our moral responsibility will only hasten our nation's demise and our own. Thus, what I hope to accomplish through this humble effort is to weigh in a moral defense worthy of our children's life-and-death struggle to save their own lives, many, sadly, too often are losing.

FOOTNOTES

[1] William Julius Wilson, *The Truly Disadvantaged: The Inner City, the Underclass, and Public Policy* (Chicago: The University of Chicago Press, 1987), p. 56. "Whereas job losses in these cities have been greatest in industries with lower educational requirements, job growth has been concentrated in industries that require higher levels of education."

[2] Sean Bell, 23, died on November 25th, a casualty of a 50-bullet spree by plain clothes NYPD policemen. See William K. Rashbaum and Al Baker, "50 Bullets, One Dead and Many Questions," *The New York Times*, December 11, 2006, B1. In Sean Bell's case, young male protesters declared Bell was executed. This might explain why officers have emptied 9-millimeter pistols and reloaded, to empty them again, in their mob-like killing sprees of young black males.

[3] When I heard the Sean Bell verdict, I became afraid for my own life, and rightly so. I'm in solidarity with Bell's undying plea for justice. His unjust shooting devalued and undervalues all black life.

[4] Many say that there were black police officers implicated in this shooting. My response to them is to wait until black police officers participate in a shooting spree of a white man, and we will then see how liberal racial politics have become in New York. They will be tried to the fullest extent of the law.

[5] Tom Hays, "Judge Clears Cops in Groom's Killing," *Associated Press*, April 25, 2008, http://news.aol.com/the-rewind/?feature=20080425155909990001&ncid=aolnws00150000000002; Internet; accessed 2 May 2008. In announcing his verdict in the non-jury trial, the judge said that "the inconsistent testimony, courtroom demeanor and rap sheets of the prosecution witnesses–mainly Bell's friends—had the effect of eviscerating" their credibility. A second chance and having paid one's debt to society means nothing; ex-offenders are still being charged with their exonerated crime.

⁶ A police state is defined as a state in which the government maintains strict control over the population, particularly through suspension of civil rights. Its objective is often to repress internal opposition among its citizens. After the enactment of the Patriot Act, some have raised concerns that the United States of America has been acquiring characteristics typical of a police state.

⁷ Lisa W. Foderaro, "Police Officer is Charged in Death of Immigrant," *The New York Times*, September 7, 2007, http://www.nytimes.com/2007/09/07/nyregion/07arrest.html; Internet; accessed 2 May 2008; In Mount Kisco, New York, a police officer beat a homeless Guatemalan immigrant to death. He was charged with second-degree manslaughter, but there had been a history of unsolved illegal immigrant deaths. Yet counties in New York are discussing expanding local police power as also immigration officers.

⁸ Kevin Powell, *Who's Gonna Take the Weight? Manhood, Race, and Power in America* (New York: Three Rivers Press, 2003), pp. 151-152.

⁹ Tupac Amara Shakur, *The Rose that Grew from Concrete* (New York: Pocket Books, 1999), 3.

¹⁰ See Kimberlé Crenshaw et al., eds, Critical Race Theory: The Key Writings That Formed the Movement (New York: The New Press, 1995).

¹¹ Richard Majors and Janet Mancini Billson, *Cool Pose: The Dilemmas of Black Manhood in America* (New York: Simon & Schuster, 1992), p. 24. "Black males, in addition to being affected by individual and group racism, are also affected by institutionalized racism, which in fact can have longer-term and more damaging effects. Institutionalized racism refers to the policies and rules, traditional practices, and informal networks that operate in major social institutions (politics, economics, and education) to keep minorities 'in their place' and out of the mainstream."

[12] The Kerner Commission's report, called the "Kerner Report," was released on February 29, 1968. One of its best known quotes was: "Our nation is moving toward two societies, one black, one white—separate and unequal."

[13] Andrew Hacker's *Two Nations: Black and White, Separate, Hostile, Unequal* was published in 1995 before Powell's 2003 *Who's Going to Take the Weight.*

[14] Andrew Hacker, *Two Nations: Black and White, Separate, Hostile, Unequal* (New York: Ballantine Books, 1995), p. 54. Actually Hacker's comments are broader than manchildren; he aims his remarks at the black race.

[15] James Bell, "Correcting The System of Unequal Justice," in *The Covenant* (Chicago: Third World Press, 2006), p. 49.

[16] See public analyst John Flateau's critical descriptive in his book, *The Prison Industrial Complex: Race, Crime & Justice in New York* (Brooklyn, New York: Medgar Evers College Press, 1996), pp. 2-3. "One can draw a number of parallels between the military industrial complex and a so-called 'prison industrial complex.' There are massive economic and political interests vested in the prison industrial complex in terms of business and employment components of prison construction, contractual services, and inmate maintenance and supervision operations. This involves all three branches of government: the executive branch, in terms of prison and law enforcement administration; the legislative branch, in terms of defining and drafting criminal laws and sanctions; and the judicial branch, in terms of sanctioning and applying criminal laws, and conducting trials and sentencing."

[17] John Flateau, *The Prison Industrial Complex: Race, Crime & Justice in New York* (Brooklyn, New York: Medgar Evers College Press, 1996), p. 12; p. 18. "Youth in the age category 16-20 years are treated as adults for the purpose of criminal prosecution."

Footnotes

[18] The bias in the criminal justice system, particularly the inequality in sentencing, has never been more apparent or more of an issue than in the correlation between race and class, on the one hand, and crack and powder cocaine, on the other. "When we get caught with five grams of crack cocaine, we get five years mandatory minimum sentencing. While 100 times more powder cocaine is a slap on the wrist." It has become appallingly apparent for those lives stolen by the sentencing process that there is a two-track system at work in the justice system. Tavis Smiley, ed., *How to Make Black America Better: Leading African Americans Speak Out* (New York, Anchor Books, 2001), p. 181.

[19] Marable, Manning. "Globalization and Racialization," *New York Beacon*, December. 6 – December. 22, 2004, p. 9.

[20] Andre Michael Eggelleton, "Behind the Headlines: 21st Century Slavery 'The Prison Industrial Complex'," *Eastside Gazette,* December 24, 2003, p. 10.

[21] Flateau, *The Prison Industrial Complex,* p. 31.

[22] Gail Russell Chaddock, "US Notches World's Highest Incarceration Rate," *Christian Science Monitor*, August 18, 2003, p. 2. The Sentencing Project is a nonprofit advocacy group based in Washington, D.C. which studies criminal-justice issues and sentencing reform.

[23] Jawanza Kunjufu, *Countering the Conspiracy to Destroy Black Boys* (Chicago: African American Images, 1995), pp. 31-55.

[24] Gary Orfield et al., "Losing our Future: How Minority Youths are being Left Behind by the Graduation Rate Crisis," [on-line]; June 2004, http://www.civilrightsproject.harvard.edu/research/dropouts/dropouts04.php#reports; Internet; accessed 1 June 2005.

[25] Bruce Western and Becky Pettit, "Beyond Crime and Punishment: Prisons and Inequality," *Ethnic NewsWatch* 1, no. 3 (Fall 2002): 37 [database on-line]; available from CUNY

Office of Library Services (Ann Arbor: ProQuest Information and Learning Company, accessed 20 November 2005); http://proquest.umi.com.

[26] Sanyika Shakur, aka Monster Kody Scott, *Monster: The Autobiography of an L.A. Gang Member* (Grove Press: New York, 1993), p. 25.

[27] Among many obstacles, the inequity made inherent to public school education is a result of the insubstantial tax base.

[28] Dierdre Glenn Paul, "Navigating the Unwieldy Terrain of Urban Education in a Post-NCLB World," *Multicultural Review*, Fall 2005, p. 39; NCLB Act wants statistics without a substantive investment in an educational resource infrastructure, not to be mixed with bureaucracy, to salvage these children's lives.

[29] Ibid., p. 40.

[30] When mothers who head single-parent households are incarcerated, the situation becomes even more alarming for black children. Children are herded into foster care, if other guardians cannot be found. This commences the vicious cycle of displacement and alienation for children, further undermining their success in life and what that means for the black community.

[31] Ernest M. Drucker, "The Impact of Mass Incarceration on Public Health in Black Communities," in *The State of Black America* (New York, National Urban League, 2003), p. 164; "The incarceration of a parent disrupts children's social environments and the financial stability of their families—weakening parental bonds and placing severe stress on the caregivers left behind. This often leads to a loss of discipline in the household, and to feelings of shame and anger in children that manifests itself in a behavioral problem in and outside of school."

[32] No conspiracy theory here, the hard data are available to legitimate such suspicions.

Footnotes

[33] Drucker, "The Impact of Mass Incarceration," p. 165.

[34] Chauncey Bailey, "Genocide or Homicide: Solutions to Stop the Madness," *Sun Reporter*, November 21, 2002, p. 1.

[35] Charles Whitaker, "Why Are Young Black Men KILLING THEMSELVES?," *Ebony*, April, 2001, p. 142.

[36] Christina Crews, "Convention to Tackle Silent Trend of Suicide," *Philadelphia Tribune*, July 25, 2000, p. 4B. "Research shows the greatest increase comes from those more likely to commit suicide: African American males age 10-24."

[37] Ibid.

[38] Kunjufu. *Countering the Conspiracy*, p. 172.

[39] Addiction is an area that this book does not adequately address, but just as important in understanding the social behavior decimating the future of young black males.

[40] M.A. Bortner and Linda M. Williams, *Youth In Prison: We the People of Unit Four* (New York: Routledge, 1997), p. 60.

[41] Ibid.

[42] Marian Wright Edelman, "Americans Should Take Stand on Criminal Treatment of Children," *Ethnic News*, July 21, 2005-July 27, 2005.

[43] Much of the economic severity being experienced in homes of black single headed households began with the 1996 Personal Responsibility and Work Opportunity Reconciliation Act, a major breach in the social safety net. The Act mandated a five-year limit to receive public assistance. Now, many of these women can't find a job to meet all of their family needs or they are working two and three jobs. In all, they are leaving their children at-risk by their absence in the home, making them vulnerable to influences outside the home as well as tension-filled stress within due to economics.

[44] Hurricane Katrina happened in August 2005 and devastated the levees of New Orleans, creating a flood and water surge that left people homeless and dead. Those who were unable to evacuate the city because of high levels of poverty were overwhelming among blacks and poor people.

[45] Barack Obama's speech at the Hampton Ministers' Conference, Hampton, Virginia, June 5, 2007, http://community. meacfans.com/eve/forums/a/tpc/f/1661044881/m/9181071583; Internet; accessed 2 May 2008.

[46] Bortner and Williams, *Youth In Prison*, p. 45.

[47] Wilson, *The Truly Disadvantaged*, p. 62; eminent sociologist William Julius Wilson, in particular, assesses a complex web of factors that inhibits their full inclusion into the American mainstream. He details such key factors as "shifts in the American economy, which have produced extraordinary rates of black joblessness that have exacerbated other social problems in the inner city—the historic flow of migrants, changes in the urban minority age structure, population changes in the central city, and the class transformation of the inner city." Wilson finds that the social web of this "concentrated effects" are systemic, institutionalized against the manchild with its superior deadly force to coerce his hand and assure him a defeated life.

[48] Ibid., p. 58. More specifically, concepts such as social buffers, concentration effects, and social isolation are used to describe the social and institutional mechanisms that aggravated enhanced patterns of social dislocations, originally caused by racial subjugation, but that have been strengthened in more recent years by such developments as the class transformation of the inner city and changes in the urban economy. See Wilson, *The Truly Disadvantaged*, 137, Concentrated effects: "The social transformation of the inner city has resulted in a disproportionate concentration of the most disadvantaged segments of the urban black population, creating a social milieu significantly different from the environment that existed in these communities several decades ago."

⁴⁹ Shakur, *Monster*, p. 118.

⁵⁰ In a fight for their lives, young black males are fighting on the frontlines of resisting the forces of global corporate capitalism that anticipates the establishment of the national security state, to which has been committed, if not by design, then by result, to feed the prison industrial complex their life blood.

⁵¹ Claude Brown, *Manchild in the Promised Land* (New York: The New American Library, 1965). Brown never said that this was his autobiography but most literary critics do acknowledge a close parallel to his life.

⁵² National Institute of Justice Homicide Trends Examined in Eight Cities, PR Newswire Association, (Washington Dateline) December 10, 1997. "In all eight cities, most homicides were committed with firearms. Guns accounted for more than 80 percent of homicides in five study cities (Detroit, Indianapolis, New Orleans, Richmond and Washington, D.C.). The proportion of homicides attributable to guns steadily increased in every study city."

⁵³ Shakur, *Monster*, p. xiii.

⁵⁴ Michael Eric Dyson, "THE LIVES THEY LIVED; Hard-Knock Lit," *The New York Times*, December 29, 2002, p. 32.

⁵⁵ Brown, *Manchild*, p. 419. Brown attended night classes at a high school downtown, left home, worked as a busboy, deliveryman and other jobs. He went on to Howard University in Washington, D.C., graduating in 1965 and later became a lawyer.

⁵⁶ Christine Brennan and Donald Huff, "Bias II: There'll Be No More 'Wait for Jay'," *The Washington Post*, December 5, 1990, p. B1; http://www.washingtonpost.com/wp-srv/sports/longterm/memories/bias/launch/jay.htm; Internet; accessed 2 May 2008.

57 Brown ended up going to night school, became a jazz pianist before leaving New York, and went to Howard University. Later, he pursued a law degree.

58 Shakur, *Monster*, p. 102.

59 Brown, *Manchild*, p. 21.

60 Ibid., p. 155.

61 Ibid., "My friends were all daring like me, tough like me, dirty like me, ragged like me, cursed like me, and had a great love for trouble like me."

62 The Freedom Writers with Erin Gruwell, *The Freedom Writers Diary: How a Teacher and 150 Teens Used Writing to Change Themselves and the World Around Them* (New York: Broadway Books, 1999), p. 15.

63 Shakur, *Monster*, p. 138.

64 Kevin Powell, *Who's Gonna Take the Weight? Manhood, Race, and Power in America* (New York: Three Rivers Press, 2003), p. 82.

65 Brown, *Manchild*, p. 176.

66 Gareth G. Davis and David B. Muhlhausen, "Young African-American Males: Continuing Victims of High Homicide Rates in Urban Communities, Center for Data Analysis Report #00-05," May 2, 2000, compiled by The Heritage Foundation, http://www.heritage.org/Research/Crime/CDA00-05.cfm; Internet, accessed 2 May 2008. This study is based upon data collected from eight of the nation's largest black urban communities: Baltimore, Maryland; Brooklyn, New York; Chicago, Illinois; Detroit, Michigan; Los Angeles, California; New Orleans, Louisiana; Philadelphia, Pennsylvania; and Washington, D.C.

67 Stephanie Banchero, "Year of violence, grief: 27 city students slain. Desolation, loss, nightmares plague those left behind at schools throughout Chicago," *Tribune*, May 16, 2007; Mary

Mitchell, "Slain boy's mom still waits for justice; 'My life changed that day,'" *Chicago Sun-Times*, May 13, 2007; Alexa Aguilar, "Thousands mourn teen 'hero' slain on CTA bus," *Tribune*, May 18, 2007.

[68] Freedom Writers, *The Freedom Writers Diary*, p. 15.

[69] Ibid., p. 16.

[70] Shakur, *Monster*, p. 17.

[71] Ibid., p. 12.

[72] Bortner and Williams, *Youth In Prison*, p. 59.

[73] Freedom Writers, *The Freedom Writers Diary*, p. 12.

[74] Brown, *Manchild*, p. 428.

[75] Freedom Writers, *The Freedom Writers Diary*, p. 25.

[76] Steven A Drizin, "Juvenile Justice System Tilted Against Minority Youths," *Chicago Daily Law Bulletin*, May 12, 2000, p. 5. "And in the case of one particular Illinois law – the automatic adult prosecution of teens caught with drugs near public housing or schools – skin color alone is driving the results and often with devastating consequences. Among the staggering statistics gleaned primarily from the Justice Department's own data, is that black youths who have never been jailed before are six times more likely to be incarcerated than white first-times who are charged with the same violent offenses"; George E. Curry, "Juveniles Get a Bad Rap," *New York Beacon*, March 28, 2001, p. 35. Cynthia Tucker, "High Rate of Black Incarceration is a Major Challenge for Us All," *Los Angeles Sentinel*, April 24, 2003, p. A6. "Among young people who have never been to a juvenile prison, blacks are more than six times as likely as whites to be sentenced by juvenile courts to prison time, according to a 2000 report, 'And Justice for Some,' issued by the Justice Department and several foundations."

[77] Bortner and Williams, *Youth In Prison*, p. xii.

[78] William Julius Wilson, *When Work Disappears: The World of the New Urban Poor* (New York: Vintage Books, 1997), p. 43. "Blacks, especially young males, are dropping out of the labor force in significant numbers. The severe problems of joblessness for black teenagers and young adults are seen in the figures on changes in the male civilian labor-force participation rates. The percentage of black males in the labor force fell sharply between 1960 and 1984 for those aged sixteen to twenty-four, and somewhat less for those aged twenty-five to thirty-four. Black males began dropping out of the labor force in increasing numbers as early as 1965, while white males either maintained or increased their rate of participation until 1981. But even these figures do not reveal the severity of joblessness among younger blacks. Only a minority of noninstitutionalized black youth are employed. ...The percentage of black male youth who are employed has sharply and steadily declined since 1955.... The fact that only 58 percent of all black young adult males, 34 percent of all black males aged eighteen to nineteen, and 16 percent of those aged sixteen to seventeen were employed in 1984 reveals a problem of joblessness for young black men has reached catastrophic proportions."

[79] Brown, *Manchild*, p. 425.

[80] Shakur, *Monster,* p. 136.

[81] Bell, *The Covenant*, p. 64.

[82] Michelle Washington, "Carjacker with a murderous past gets life in prison," *The Virginian-Pilot*, December 22, 2007, p. B1.

[83] Bortner and Williams, *Youth In Prison*, p. 148; Bell, *The Covenant,* pp. 47-69.

[84] Social death is a term used to describe the condition of estrangement and disenfranchisement endured by certain populations within a wider society.

[85] In the near future is the shift to corporate partnerships or privatization.

[86] Tamara E. Holmes, "Incarceration Rates Fuel Economic Crisis," *Black Enterprise*, August 2003, p. 22.

[87] Glen Ford and Peter Gamble, "America's Gulag: The Mass Incarceration of African Americans," *The Broward Times*, April 2, 2004, p. 10. When we speak of the American gulag, the systematic incarceration of a population little valued for extermination and disposability.

[88] Ibid.

[89] Ibid.

[90] Christopher D. Benson, "Dealing With The Exploding Prison Population," *Ebony*, December 2003, p. 128.

[91] The Sentencing Project, "Felony Disenfranchisement Laws in the United States," http://www.sentencingproject.org/pdfs/1046.pdf; Internet, accessed, 4 September 2007; P. Thomas, "Study Suggests Black Male Prison Rate Impinges on Political Process," *The Washington Post*, January 30, 1997, p. A3.

[92] Brown, *Manchild*, p. 184.

[93] Nathan McCall, *Makes Me Wanna Holler: A Young Black Man in America* (New York: Vintage Books, 1995), p. 214. He was incarcerated for armed robbery and served three- years of a twelve-year term. Eventually, he became a journalist at the *Washington Post*.

[94] Soon *Law & Order* will re-try the case with its liberal justice to set the social wrongs right. But that's only television. What about real life redemption for these young men?

[95] Patrice Gaines, "After A Violent Death," *Essence*, July 1994, p. 36.

[96] Stephanie Heinatz, "A Mother's Nightmare," *The Virginian-Pilot*, March 6, 2005, p. A14.

⁹⁷ Lonise Bias was the mother of two sons who died untimely deaths: the Boston Celtic's rookie superstar Len Bias, who died an untimely death from drug overdose trauma, and a younger son, nineteen-year-old Jay Bias, shot- to- death following an argument at a Prince George's County mall in Maryland.

⁹⁸ See the argument for racial realism: Derrick A. Bell, "Racial Realism," in *Critical Race Theory: The Key Writings that Formed the Movement*, eds., Kimberlé Crenshaw et al., (New York: The New Press, 1995), p. 308. "I am convinced that there is something real out there in America for black people. It is not, however, the romantic love of integration; it is surely not the long-sought goal of equality under law, though we must maintain the struggle against racism, else the erosion of black rights will become even worse than it is now. The Racial Realism that we must seek is simply a hard-eyed view of racism as it is and our subordinate role in it. We must realize, as our slave forebears did, that the struggle for freedom is, at bottom, a manifestation of our humanity which survives and grows stronger through resistance to oppression, even if that oppression is never overcome."

⁹⁹ On Monday, August 6, 2007, four young people were shot execution-style in Newark, New Jersey: Terrance Aerial,18; Iofemi Hightower, 20; and Dashon Harvey, 20; but Natasha Aerial, 19 survived the attack.

¹⁰⁰ Toni Morrison, "The World According to Toni Morrison," *Essence*, May 1995, p. 222.

¹⁰¹ This is an excerpt from Governor George Wallace's 1962 oath of office speech: "In the name of the greatest people that have ever trod this earth, I draw the line in the dust and toss the gauntlet before the feet of tyranny, and I say segregation now, segregation tomorrow, segregation forever." Later the following year, June 11, 1963, Governor Wallace barred the doors of the University of Alabama to integration.

¹⁰² D. Glaister, "Abort all Black Babies and Court Crime, says Republican." *The Guardian*, October 1, 2005, p. 14.

[103] Ibid. "With the kind of so-called Republican moralism, our finest elected officials have not been able to stand the test of integrity with all of their advantages in life. And yet, black youth must pay dearly for sins that have never amounted to the corruption of a nation."

[104] Ibid.

[105] In this case, rather than a call for outright, full-fledged genocide, Bennett's remarks were constrained to eugenics. Eugenics advocates the improvement of humanity through controversial methods, such as state-sponsored discrimination, forced sterilization of persons deemed racially or genetically defective, and the killing of institutionalized populations. Its career in human history has always coveted a fair amount of suspicions and judgment because it tends to prey upon the vulnerability of certain populations considered disposable or powerless. On the other hand, genocide a term more assertive in language, is deliberate or not so deliberate, but achieves the same results and is the systematic destruction, killing, extermination of an ethnic, racial, religious, or national group.

[106] Preemptive strike was a doctrine espoused by President Bush after 9/11 to serve notice to potential enemy combatants that the United States would not hesitate to strike at any imminent danger first.

[107] Paul Robeson and William L. Patterson, eds., "We Charge Genocide: The Crime of Government Against the Negro People," presented to the United Nations in December 1951.

[108] Glaister, "Abort all Black Babies," p. 14.

[109] Bortner and Williams, *Youth In Prison*, p. 176.

[110] Chris Holmes, "My Friends Aren't Monsters; Three Young, Black Males, Good Citizens All- Reflect on Crime, Stereotypes and a Society They Consider Hostile to Them and their Peers," *St Louis Post –Dispatch*, January 17, 1996, p. 1E.

[111] Wilson, *The Truly Disadvantaged*, pp. 61-62. Sociologist William J. Wilson debates the efficacy of a culture of poverty and supplants this idea with the theoretical concept of social isolation. As he theorizes it, the black poor confined to the geography of the inner-city have experienced a pervasive social isolationism from mainstream job practices, mores, values, and norms. As a result, their behavior has not adapted to what mainstream society considers normative. That social isolation has inhered values non-productive to assimilating within mainstream society, especially where the world of work is considered. While Wilson's argument does not embrace a biological or social determinism through the front door, though the descriptive differs, still a "culture of poverty" or "values" of poverty gets inserted through the back door. Rather than any inherent deficit on the part of the inner-city poor, value deficit results from a systemic engineering, instigated by job displacement and middle-and working-class inner-city abandonment. The minor role of race is allowed to "contribut[e] to the increasing social and economic woes of the ghetto underclass." Race alone, in his opinion, is too simplified an argument; it must be located with the complex of social factors engineering young black male mass unemployment, incarceration, and disenfranchisement. However, the role of race in explaining the racialization of poverty is subordinated to the harsh forces of neoliberal economics and racial desertion. As much as we all seek to retire race from the ensuing discourse, which has performed its job well in giving explanation to the inequalities that prevent full participation of blacks, it cannot go quietly into a slumbered state. It still possesses too much analytic currency in deconstructing social, economic, and political inequities. In other words, too much social reality still breaks down along the lines of race to empty it of its analytic value. How the various analytic categories act opportunistically to reinforce the racialization of poverty is of more concern to me. Lastly, how thick is the isolationism that Wilson proposes, which drives the development of norms, values, and practices antithetical to so-called mainstream culture? I propose that it's relatively thin, given how inner-city culture has so easily embraced the violence, misogyny, sexism, rabid materialism,

and consumerism synonymous with mainstream culture. The irony is that this pervasive isolationism, he proposes, has had the uncanny ability to be penetrated by some of the worst mainstream practices. His thesis suggests that through public policy remedies, such as job training programs and education initiatives, that the counterproductive behavior manifested by young men can be transformed into potential. "From a public-policy perspective, this would mean shifting the focus from changing subcultural traits (as suggested by the "culture of poverty" thesis) to changing the structure of constraints and opportunities." Many still question, without attention to race, can public policy remedies yield significant results? At the same time, I must confess that his argument for the truly disadvantaged is encouraging and rings with a clarity of truth that cannot be dismissed.

[112] William J. Bennett et al., *Body Count: Moral Poverty...and How to Win America's War Against Crime and Drugs* (New York: Simon & Schuster, 1996), p. 13. "By 'moral poverty' we mean the poverty of being without loving, capable, responsible adults who teach the young right from wrong. It is the poverty of being without parents, guardians, relatives, friends, teachers, coaches, clergy, and others who *habituate*...children to feel joy at others' joy; pain at others' pain; satisfaction when you do right; remorse when you do wrong."

[113] Don Terry, "United States: Murder-suicides of Teen Gang Members Shake 'Happy Valley,'" *The Ottawa Citizen*, June 28, 1995, p. A9.

[114] Drucker, "The Impact of Mass Incarceration, p.154. The relationship is made of crime rates to the economy. As unemployment soars, so have crime rates.

[115] Roger Clegg, "Race and Crime," 161 *New Jersey Law Journal*, 324, July 24, 2000, p. 24.

[116] Once the head of Bush's faith-based initiative, John Dilulio co-wrote with William Bennett and John Walters, Dilulio suggests that "a late 1990s juvenile-crime explosion will be

driven by a rising tide of …deeply troubled young men." He had earlier "attracted uncritical attention from the left and the right for his talk of the growth of a 'super-predator' caste of feral young males born of the absence of civil society, families, and churches in many parts of America." Excerpted from "The Real John Dilulio" by Eli Lehrer of The Heritage Foundation, February 7, 2001, archived at http://www.heritage.org; Internet, accessed, 2 May 2008.

[117] Bennett, *Body Count*, p. 45.

[118] Ibid., p. 27. Definition provided: "super-predators: radically impulsive, brutally remorseless youngsters, including ever more preteenage boys, who murder, assault, rape, rob, burglarize, deal deadly drugs, join gun-toting gangs, and create serious communal disorders. They do not fear the stigma of arrest, the pains of imprisonment, or the pangs of conscience…. To these mean-street youngsters, the words, 'right' and 'wrong' have no fixed moral meaning."

[119] Glaister, "Abort all Black Babies," p. 14.

[120] Bennett, *Body Count*, p. 14.

[121] Ibid., pp. 15-16.

[122] Evelyn Brooks Higginbotham, *Righteous Discontent: The Women's Movement in the Black Baptist Church, 1880-1920* (Cambridge: Harvard University Press, 1993), 190. "From the days of slavery, well into the twentieth century, widespread assumptions of the black woman's innate promiscuity prevented legal redress in the case of her victimization by rape."

[123] This type of scapegoating can occur if a nation is obsessed enough with its own survival fears to inflict the necessary sacrificial violence, endemic to western doctrines of divine favor or manifest destiny, sometimes mystified in religious language of election and atonement. Although representing a different time and place in history, western history is almost a re-enactment of the roots of Christian history and its bleeding

Footnotes

crucifixes. René Girard, *The Scapegoat*, trans. Yvonne Freccero (Baltimore: Johns Hopkins University Press, 1986).

[124] Wilson, *Disappear*, p. xiii.

[125] Wilson, *The Truly Disadvantaged*, p. 62.

[126] Americans see the flagrant disregard President Bush has for the civil liberties of Americans with his fervent push for wire taps and bypassing the Foreign Intelligence Surveillance Court (FISC), as well as refusing to abide by the law in interrogation techniques. American citizens and our children see a rogue presidency and take heart from that kind of vigilanteeism to execute their own reign of terror upon fellow citizens with impunity. Look at this new law in Texas where citizens can shoot one another, guilty or innocent; the law has been subordinated to the control of individuals without due process.

[127] A January 1999 Report from the U.S. Department of Justice, Office of Justice Program, Bureau of Justice Statistics, "Homicide Trends in the United States," suggests recent declines among young black youth.

[128] Flateau, *The Prison Industrial Complex*, p. 3.

[129] Joy James, ed., *The Angela Y. Davis Reader* (New York: Blackwell Publishing, 1998), p. 65.

[130] Eggelleton, "Behind the Headlines," p. 6. "Legislation and individual accountability need our attention. The disproportionate sentencing guidelines for powder and crack cocaine are a glaring example of the structural racism permeating the American justice system. About 90 percent of crack arrests are of African Americans, while 75 percent of powder cocaine arrests are of whites. Under federal law, it takes only five grams of crack cocaine to trigger a five-year mandatory minimum sentence. It takes 500 grams of powder cocaine to get this same sentence. To date, Congress has refused to change these disproportional sentencing laws."

[131] James, ed., *The Angela Davis Reader*, p. 67.

[132] I do believe W.E.B. Dubois would be quite comfortable in my asserting that black masculinity also labors under a punitive double consciousness in America, which indebts it to the very forces it seeks to overthrow to discover his own true self-consciousness.

[133] Cornel West, *Race Matters* (Vintage Books: New York, 1993), pp. 124-125.

[134] To reiterate the lynch history of black men should not obfuscate the lynch history of black women and children.

[135] At a high school in Jena, Louisiana, there was a "white tree," where it was an unspoken rule that it was for white students only. Black students sat under the tree to defy the blatant ritual of segregation and racism. The next day, three ropes tied to nooses were displayed to instill fear in the black students who sat under the tree. The scene played out where 16-year-old Mychal Bell was arrested along with five others, making them the Jena 6. These manchildren were railroaded by a district attorney who had no evidence that these youth deserved imprisonment, but to send a strong message of fear through the black community that white supremacy still reigns sixty years after civil rights protest and Jim Crow abolition.

[136] Crews, "Convention to Tackle Silent, p. 48. "We stress 'leave no child behind,' but as soon as they become youth and young adults we criticize and demonize them…. We call them super predators and wild wolf packs. What that does is create a social and cultural index that makes them think "I'm on my own. There's no one out there for me' so it conditions their attitude and their life expectancy."

[137] Majors and Billson, *Cool Pose*, p. 24. "Institutionalized racism refers to the policies and rules, traditional practices, and informal networks that operate in major social institutions (politics, economics, and education) to keep minorities 'in their place' and out of the mainstream."

[138] See Tuesday, July 24, 2008, CNN Special on "Plight of the Black Man in America"; http://www.cnn.com/SPECIALS/2008/black.in.america.

[139] Bell, *The Covenant*, p. 54.

[140] The trend is as such that it's less the judge's decision, but prosecutors are making these decisions about youth's fate.

[141] Black men return to boys in the criminal justice system. They are placed under supervision of the state as recalcitrant children. Still they cannot claim a mature destiny.

[142] Camille O. Cosby, "Camille Cosby: America Taught my Son's Killer to Hate Blacks," *USA Today*, July 8 1998, p. 15A.

[143] "Nigger" was always to disparage the less than human status of the black race, assigned by white power relations in America.

[144] At the 98th National Association for the Advancement of Colored People, a symbolic ceremony was staged to bury the n-word by the youth contingent on the board of directors. Black youth must understand the spirit of blasphemy that produced this term, and no matter how much we brag about how black youth are inverting its original sacrilege of black humanity, it still bears the repulse of its original sin.

[145] David Walker, 1785-1830; *Walker's Appeal, in Four Articles; Together with a Preamble, to the Coloured Citizens of the World, but in Particular, and Very Expressly, to Those of the United States of America, Written in Boston, State of Massachusetts*, September 28, 1829.

[146] That portrayal of pre-sixties social relations is not quite true to life; probably, the more of a liberal extreme than the common, everyday injuries to black identity, figured most pronounced in the language of "girl" or "boy." But the audience, nevertheless, gains some sense of the refusal of black humanity.

[147] Paul Laurence Dunbar wrote the poem, "We Wear the Mask."

[148] Alton Maddox, *The New York Amsterdam News*, December 22-28, 2005, p. 12-13.

[149] Powell, *Who's Gonna Take the Weight*, p. 100.

[150] Ford and Gamble, "America's Gulag," p. 10. "Mass incarceration was the national response to the civil-rights and Black Power movements, a white societal reaction to black intrusions into white 'space.' The incarceration frenzy shows no signs of letting up."

[151] Marcus Aurelius Garvey's U.N.I.A. (Universal Negro Improvement Association).

[152] Malcolm X and Alex Haley, *The Autobiography of Malcolm X* (New York: Grove Press, 1965), p. 11. Malcolm held suspicions that his father's death was not a suicide as declared by the local authority but an execution of a strong black man.

[153] Haki Madhubuti, *Black Men: Obsolete, Single, Dangerous?* (Chicago: Third World Press, 1990), p. 190.

[154] This is no argument for the efficacy of patriarchy and its accrued privileges or of its necessity for the advancement of the survival interest of black people. My argument is premised on the double standard that has evolved due to race relations in America. For instance, in the white community, the male has been pedestralized as the quintessential man or male while the black man has been infantilized and vilified as the "boy," the rapist, or the deadbeat dad. Even as I make this argument, I am quite cognizant of the privileges that black males have exercised because of their gender, including their oppressive sexism against black women's freedom, empowerment and equal rights and opportunities.

[155] Powell, *Who's Gonna Take the Weight*, p. 57

[156] Tragically, lacking fatherly role-models in their minds make every male a potential predator, even grandfather figures. Preying upon the elderly by our youth has increased significantly in the black community.

[157] Powell, *Who's Gonna Take the Weight*, p. 158.

[158] Majors and Billson, *Cool Pose*, p. 17.

[159] Ellis Cose, *The Envy of The World: On Being A Black Man In America* (New York: Washington Square Press, 2002), pp. 161-2.

[160] Brutalizing women cannot be chalked up to a typical male bonding ritual or game "sport." Prosecuted as a crime, domestic abuse, violation and/or rape subjugation of black women harms the black community, and will never be honored, legitimated or validated as appropriate masculinity.

[161] Haki R. Madhubuti, *Claiming Earth: Race, Rage, Rape, Redemption* (Chicago: Third World Press, 1994), pp. 148-9.

[162] See Richard Majors and Janet Mancini Billson, *Cool Pose: The Dilemmas of Black Manhood in America* (New York: Simon & Schuster, 1992). Social scientists are acknowledging that too much research done on the black family evolves from Moynihan's concept of the pathological and antisocial black matriarchal family and its ostensibly negative impact on the ego development of black males. The call is for more research that assesses the factors of race, class, gender and socioeconomic forces in shaping and defining masculinity among black males.

[163] No one supports any perspective that black families don't need male participants and role-models. They do. But casting the blame on black women for their absence and lack of participation is where the reasoning of Moynihan and I part company.

[164] Author Michelle Wallace's critique of that superwoman myth is found in her controversial text *Black Macho and the Myth of the Black Superwoman*; see Michelle Wallace, *Black Macho and the Myth of the Black Superwoman* (New York: Dial Press, 1979).

[165] Majors and Billson, *Cool Pose*, p. 33.

[166] bell hooks, *We Real Cool: Black Men and Masculinity* (New York: Routledge, 2004), p. 104.

[167] Shakur, *Monster*, p. 163.

[168] The 2001 No Child Left Behind Act (NCLB) authorizes a number of federal programs directed to improve the performance of school children by increasing standards of accountability for states, school districts, and schools. In these latter days, it has come under heavy criticism of its shortcomings.

[169] Deborah Prothrow-Stith and Michaele Weissman, *Deadly Consequences/How Violence Is Destroying Our Teenage Population and a Plan to Begin Solving the Problem* (New York: Harper Collins Publishers, 1991), p. 79.

[170] Kunjufu, *Countering the Conspiracy,* p. 185.

[171] A conservative count places it as high as six (6) hours a day of black children watching television. And although commercial messages are becoming subtler, their intent is still unmistakably clear.

[172] Isaiah Washington, "For a Black Man, Acting Can Be a Drag," *Essence*, June 1996, p. 34.

[173] February 2006 in New York City. McDonald's featured a black couple, situated with the male partner making changes to their home that included several women. He introduced his wife to these changes with her saying, "I hope you like what you did to the doghouse." He responds, "We don't have a dog." And she looks at him tellingly as if to say, "you're the dog."

[174] Manfred B. Steger, *Globalization: A Very Short Introduction* (Oxford: Oxford University Press, 2003), pp. 76-77. "In 2000, only ten media conglomerates- AT&T, Sony, AOL/Time Warner, Bertelsmann, Liberty Media, Vivendi Universal, Viacom, General Electric, Disney, and News Corporation –accounted

for more than two-thirds of the $250-275 billion in annual worldwide revenues generated by the communications industry.... Today, most media analysts concede that the emergence of a global commercial-media market amounts to the creation of a global oligopoly similar to what of the oil and automotive industries in the early part of the 20ᵗʰ century. The crucial cultural innovators of earlier decades – small, independent record labels, radio stations, movie theatres, newspapers, and book publishers – have become virtually extinct as they found themselves incapable of competing with the media giant."

[175] Ibid.

[176] This is no effort to pander to homophobic biases either.

[177] Dave Chappelle first left *Comedy Central* in May 2005. He was interviewed on the Oprah Show, Feb. 3, 2006.

[178] Shell, BP, Exxon Mobil, Chevron and Total recently received oil contracts in Iraq according to CNN, Monday, June 30, 2008. This confirms criticism that the Iraq war was largely about western interest in oil.

[179] Frantz Fanon, *Black Skin, White Masks* (New York: Grove Press, 1967), p. 159.

[180] Frances Cress Welsing, *The Isis Papers: The Keys to the Colors* (Chicago: Third World Press, 1991), p. 84.

[181] Michelle Nealy, "Diverse Issues in Higher Education," *Black Issues in Higher Education*, August 25, 2005, p. 26.

[182] Black sitcoms are where I have seen this kind of ideological attack upon icons of black resistance most noticeably.

[183] Any study of significance in American society about black life or history fundamentally has been authorized and legitimized by white authors, from Gunnar Myrdal's *The American Dilemma* to Richard Kluger's *Simple Justice* to David Garrow's documenting of the life and work of Dr. Martin Luther King, Jr.

[184] Greg Mathis, "Feds should fund gun violence projects," *Tri-State Defender*. July 16-20, 2005, p. 4A.

[185] Davis and Muhlhausen, "Young African-American Males," May 2, 2000.

[186] Ibid.

[187] Ibid.

[188] Juvenile Offenders and Victims 2006 National Report.

[189] Earl Ofari Hutchinson, *The Assassination of the Black Male Image* (New York: Simon & Schuster, 1996), p. 31.

[190] Temporary Assistance for Needy Families (TANF) is the newest invention of aid to single mothers and their children.

[191] In the black community, seventy percent of the families are headed by single females.

[192] Since 1970, women and children account for an increasing number falling below the poverty line. A significant number of these women are divorced or never-married mothers. – "Juveniles who lived with both biological parents had lower lifetime prevalence of law-violating behaviors than did juveniles who lived in other family types."

[193] Shakur, *Monster*, p. 103.

[194] Prothrow-Stith and Weissman, *Deadly Consequences*, p. 16.

[195] Bailey, "Genocide or Homicide," p. 1.

[196] Stephanie Banchero, "Year of violence, grief: 27 city students slain. Desolation, loss, nightmares plague those left behind at schools throughout Chicago," *Tribune*, May 16, 2007; Mary Mitchell, "Slain boy's mom still waits for justice; 'My life changed that day,'" *Chicago Sun-Times*, May 13, 2007; Alexa Aguilar, "Thousands mourn teen 'hero' slain on CTA bus," *Tribune,* May 18, 2007.

[197] Lisa Jones, Bulletproof Diva: Tales of Race, Sex and Hair (NY: Doubleday, 1997), p. 179.

[198] Marilyn Jones, "Journey Toward Peace," Christian Science Sentinel, December 13, 2004, p. 8.

[199] Earl Byrd. "#205: Teen Murder Just Another Number," Afro-American Red Star, November 1, 2002, p. A1.

[200] Gaines, "After A Violent Death," p. 36.

[201] Herbert Dyer, Jr. "Why We Need Father Figures," Essence, June 1992, p. 132.

[202] Powell, Who's Gonna Take the Weight, p. 76

[203] The Juvenile Offenders and Victims 2006 National Report.

[204] At the federal level, when Homeland Security initiates curfews, American citizens should see that as the beginning of the end of civil liberties once enjoyed by a democratic nation. Be assured the war of terror will transition this nation into something anti-democratic with the scary emergence of a police state.

[205] Barbara White Stack, "It's All There in Black and White: Racial, institutional bias compound the damage inflicted by a flawed law," Pittsburgh Post-Gazette, March 18, 2001, p. A-10.

[206] Mandatory sentence is a court decision setting where judicial discretion is limited by law. Typically, people convicted of certain crimes must be punished with at least a minimum number of years in prison.

[207] Cynthia Tucker, "Black Males' Lock in Jail Time Threatens Us All," The Atlanta Journal-Constitution, April 20, 2003, p. 10C.

[208] Ryan Davis, "Study: 1 in 5 young black city men in jail; 52 percent are in prison or on parole or probation," The Baltimore Sun, March 15, 2005, p. 1B.

[209] Earl Ofari Hutchinson, "Felon Ban Continues to Hurt Blacks and Democrats," Atlanta Daily World, February 24, 2005 – March 2, 2005, p. 10.

[210] Jawanza Kunjufu, "Where are all the Black Men," The Jacksonville Free Press, Jan 16, 2002, p. 3.

[211] Ibid.

[212] Randall G. Shelden and William B. Brown. "America's New Apartheid," The Broward Times, July 23 - July 29, 2004, p. 8.

[213] Ford and Gamble, "America's Gulag," p. 10.

[214] Drucker, "The Impact of Mass Incarceration," p. 165.

[215] Drizin, "Juvenile justice system tilted against minority youths," p. 5.

[216] Ibid; Bell, The Covenant, p. 54.

[217] Shelden and Brown, "America's New Apartheid," p. 8.

[218] Bell, The Covenant, p. 54.

[219] Daniel Gray, "New Studies Point to Crisis Among African-American Men," The Tennessee Tribune. May 5 - May 11, 2005, p. 13A.

[220] Bell, The Covenant, p. 53.

[221] Ibid.

[222] Hutchinson, "Felon Ban Continues," p. 10.

[223] The prison population can only continue to grow with mandatory minimum sentencing laws, which require inmates to serve a specified proportion of their time behind bars; truth-in-sentencing laws, which require an inmate to actually serve the time he was sentenced to; and a variety of three-strikes laws increasing the penalties for repeated offenders.

Footnotes

[224] David Nyhan, "Bumper-sticker Prison Reform," *The Boston Globe*, December 6, 1995, p. 23.

[225] Benson, "Dealing With the Exploding Prison Population," p. 128.

[226] Linn Washington, Jr., "Holmesburg prisoners were human guinea pigs," *Philadelphia Tribune*, May 26, 1998, p. 2A. "Pennsylvania had more prisons with testing than anywhere in this country....But Holmesburg exceeded any place else in the number of prisoners tested and the number of years of experimentation."

[227] K. Chandler, "Prisoners to start being used for drug trials, medical experiments, if government has its way," *Westside Gazette*, September 21-September 27, 2006, p. 4A.

[228] See Allen Hornblum, *Acres of Skin* (New York: Routledge, 1998).

[229] Washington, "Holmesburg prisoners were human guinea pigs," p. 2-A.

[230] Ibid.

[231] Chandler. "Prisoners to start being used for drug trials," p. 4A.

[232] In the present war in Iraq, a criminal or drug record is waived to accept recruits into the U.S. military.

[233] Tuesday, Oct. 3, 2007 the hearing took place before the House Committee on Oversight and Government Reform.

[234] The Dream Act is a bill that would grant citizenship to illegal immigrant students who meet special stipulation.

[235] Michelle Nealy, "National Urban League Panel Says Incarceration Most Serious Issue Facing Black Males," *Diverse Issues in Higher Education*. August 25, 2005, p. 26.

[236] Bell, *The Covenant*, p. 53.

[237] Nealy, "National Urban League Panel Says Incarceration Most Serious Issue Facing Black Males," p. 26.

[238] In many states, prisoners lose the right to vote; sometimes never to be restored.

[239] The Sentencing Project, "Felony Disenfranchisement Laws in the United States," http://www.sentencingproject.org/pdfs/1046.pdf, September 2007; P. Thomas, "Study Suggests Black Male Prison Rate Impinges on Political Process," *The Washington Post*, January 30, 1997, p. A3.

[240] In February 1999, four New York City policemen searching for a rape suspect knocked on Amadou Diallo's door to question him.

[241] Charles Whitaker, "Why Are Young Black Men KILLING THEMSELVES?" *Ebony*, April, 2001, p. 142.

"Suicide by cop" is not the concept I am employing here to explain the death of Timothy Stansbury. However, it's close definition to what I'm discussing, and therefore, demanded some clarity. "Suicide by cop" makes it so difficult to place blame, that it must be utilized advisedly or young black males will have one more strike used against them to justify their homicide by agents of law and order. Some social scientists believe that a fraction of the Black youths killed in showdowns with law enforcement officials are also engaged in a form of self-destruction dubbed 'suicide by cop'."

[242] James Byrd was killed in Jasper, Texas in 1998, as a result of being knifed in the throat and dragged to bits.

[243] William Cosby, "DR BILL COSBY SPEAKS: at the 50th Anniversary commemoration of the Brown vs Topeka Board of Education Supreme Court Decision," Monday, May 17, 2004, www.eightcitiesmap.com/transcript_bc.htm, 9/7/2007; Ernie Suggs, "Cosby a lightning rod in debate over black culture," *Cox News Service*, November 17, 2004.

Footnotes

[244] Ibid.

[245] In all truth, I feel for Cosby. He is afraid of the sniper–like conditions threatening the perpetuity of the black community. He is afraid that this present generation cannot be trusted to carry on the hard-won legacy in blood of generations before them. He is afraid that the community he once cherished no longer exists except in the memory of our hearts.

[246] Cosby, "DR BILL COSBY SPEAKS," Monday, May 17, 2004.

[247] Jesse L. Jackson. "Open Letter: Harsh Criticism of Dr. Bill Cosby," *Miami Times*, August 16-August 22, 2006, p. 3A.

[248] George E. Curry, "Bill Cosby Stands Behind Critical Comments," *Atlanta Daily News*, May 27, 2007, http://www.zwire.com/site/news.cfm?newsid=11810453&BRD=1077&PAG=461&dept_id=237827&rfi=6.

[249] Jackson, "Open Letter," p. 3A.

[250] Michael Eric Dyson, *Is Bill Cosby Right?: Or Has the Black Middle Class Lost Its Mind?* (New York: Basic Civitas Books, 2005), p. 219.

[251] Ibid., pp. 219-220.

[252] Cosby, "DR BILL COSBY SPEAKS," Monday, May 17, 2004.

[253] Wilson, *Truly Disadvantaged*, p. 56.

[254] Ibid.

[255] Ibid.

[256] Robert M. Franklin, *Crisis in the Village* (Minneapolis: Fortress Press, 2007), pp. 217-243.

[258] Dyson, *Is Bill Cosby Right?*, p. 4. "Cosby bypassed, or, more accurately, short-circuited, the policing mechanism the black elite—the Aristocracy—habitually use to keep such thoughts from public view. (This is done not so much to spare the poor but to save the black elite from further embarrassment. And no matter how you judge Cosby's comments you can't help but believe that a great deal of his consternation with the poor stems from his desire to remove the shame he feels in their presence and about their activities in the world.)"

[259] Ibid., p. xiv. "The black poor—the Ghettocracy—consists of the desperately unemployed and underemployed, those trapped in underground economies, and those working poor folk who slave in menial jobs at the edge of the economy. The Ghettocracy is composed of single mothers on welfare, single working mothers and fathers, poor fathers, married poor and working folk, the incarcerated, and a battalion of impoverished children. Ironically enough, the Ghettocracy extends into the ranks of athletes and entertainers—especially basketball and football players, but, above all, hip-hop stars—whose values and habits are alleged to be negatively influenced by their poor origins. Thus, the conflict between the Afristocracy and the Ghettocracy takes on generational overtones, since the values and behaviors that are detested by Afristocrats are largely—though by no means exclusively—located among the young."

[260] See Derrick Bell, *Faces At the Bottom of the Well: The Permanence of Racism* (New York: Basic Books, 1992).

[261] This rapper is referring to selling crack cocaine, drugs, or one has to be a very good basketball athlete who can make it to the NBA.

[262] Wilson, *The Truly Disadvantaged*, p. 56. "More specifically, I believe that the exodus of middle- and working- class families from many ghetto neighborhoods removes an important 'social buffer' that could deflect the full impact of the kind of prolonged and increasing joblessness that plagued inner-city neighborhoods in the 1970s and early 1980, joblessness created by uneven economic growth and periodic recessions. This

argument is based on the assumption that even if the truly disadvantaged segments of an inner-city area experience a significant increase in long-term spells of joblessness, the basic institutions in that area (churches, schools, stores, recreational facilities, etc.) would remain viable if much of the base of their support comes from the more economically stable and secure families."

[263] Prothrow-Stith and Weissman, *Deadly Consequences*, p. 83.

[264] Bell, *Silent Covenant*, p. 200. Definition of racial fortuity: "In our anxiety to identify, we are attracted to the obvious and the superficial, the least worthy characteristics of the dominant group. It is that unconscious component of quest that gives even hard-earned progress a mirage-like quality. The decision in Brown and all the civil rights recognitions that came before— for there were far more recognitions of racial injustices than meaningful remedies—seemed more real than they could possibly be. We hardly noticed that the advances we hailed actually marked those periods when policymakers realized that remedies for racial injustice and the nation's needs coincided. Fortuity was more important than any national commitment to 'freedom and justice for all.'"

[265] Ibid., p. 8.

[266] Ibid., p. 181.

[267] Dyson, *Is Bill Cosby Right*, p. 198, "The philosophy of racial uplift, dating back to the nineteenth century, rests on the belief among black elites that the lower classes of black folk had to be roped in before their moral lapses gave white folk even more reason to repress black life." In his definition, Dyson uses strong language to overly characterize or caricature that which comes to the black community with much nuance and interpretative overlay. Yes, he does a generous critique of the elitism inherent to the articulation and practice of this particular philosophy

dated back to the nineteenth century. The points he makes are fair and pointed, but I'm unsure in his final analysis whether he is dismissive of this centuries-old practice as hopelessly flawed and useless, its purpose ambivalent. Indeed, there is a jaded side to 'lifting as we climb' but taken from a different perspective, it has operated as an interventionist strategy in the life of a community under siege, no matter how inadequate. The survival of the community was at stake, and not on their terms. Furthermore, I'm not convinced that every middle-and-upper-class person who practiced 'lifting as we climb' was committed to the demoralization of the black masses or felt they represented little redemptive value. Nannie Helen Burroughs and Mary McCleod Bethune, to me, do not represent elitism in their interaction with poor black women and people, but advocates of their possibility and that of their children in a segregated society or within the narrow confines of black high society. Black churches and black church women, central to the mainstreaming of 'lifting as we climb,' were not perfect by any means, but unwavering in their diligence to save each generation. With his collapsing of this social philosophy under the menacing elitism of the Afristocracy, has Dyson only done a masculinist reading that a womanist reading would dispute and find wanting? And even as he raises the name of sociologist Evelyn Higginbotham whose book, *Righteous Discontent*, presents primary research on this subject, to me, he does not do her findings justice. I also think the work of sociologist Cheryl Gilkes, in *If It Wasn't for the Women,* is just as compelling and vital in providing a womanist reading of black religious women's activism and service. Just because the carrying out of their benevolence fell far short of its positive aim, does that make the Good Samaritan's intentions worthless? The jury is still out. Because after all of Dyson's castigation of black middle class virtue, tell me how are we to compete in American society without adopting some of their values, like education, to compete for success? Finally, has Dyson given some an excuse, a way out, that will come to a no-good-end?

Footnotes

[268] Bakari Kitwana, The Hip Hop Generation: Young Blacks and The Crisis in African-American Culture (New York: Basic Civitas Books, 2002), p. 184.

[269] Oprah Winfrey, "The O Interview Presents Oprah Talks to Denzel Washington," O: The Oprah Magazine, January 2008, p. 214.

[270] Cosby, "DR BILL COSBY SPEAKS," Monday, May 17, 2004.

[271] Juan Williams, Enough: The Phony Leaders, dead-End Movements, and Culture of Failure That Are Undermining Black America—and What We Can Do About It (New York: Crown, 2006), p. 213. At this point, I'm clear that his conservativism regarding institutional remedies might not fairly address the increasing Hobbesian nature of our society, especially with this new global economy. Rethinking the social safety net is not to say remove it altogether.

[272] This comes out of the ongoing debate sparked by Bill Cosby with the speech he gave at the 50th Anniversary commemoration of the Brown vs the Board of Education sponsored by the National Association of the Advancement of Colored People (NAACP).

[273] Stanley Crouch, "Updating Our Battles," in How to Make Black America Better: Leading African Americans Speak Out, ed. Tavis Smiley (New York, Anchor Books, 2001), 95.

*

Association, The New York City Administration for Children's Services, Exodus Transitional Community, City Year of New York, Teachers College-Columbia University, United Way of New York, Public Private Ventures, National Basketball Players Association and Medgar Evers College.

[274] This article evolved also from a conversation with Rev. C. Vernon Mason at the Uth Turn Headquarters.

[275] Sixty percent black and 40 percent Hispanic make-up the program.

[276] The Bethany program is now an independent model.

*

2008. Sources consulted: Insideschools.org, Thursday, October 20, 2005; Art McFarland "Eagle Academy, Revisited," March 24, 2008, http://www.nycenet.edu/hs_directory/2004-05/bronx/ EAGLE%20ACADEMY%20FOR%20YOUNG%20MEN.pdf; "Comments from Young Men of how this school is making a difference"; Lynda Richardson, "For Principal, New Boys' School Is a Call to Action," New York Times, September 23, 2004, http://www.coveringeducation.org/schoolstories/boysschool.html; Elisabeth Hulette, Single-sex Schools and Minority Achievement: Eagle Academy Takes on the 'Crisis' of Inner City Boys," http://www.coveringeducation.org/schoolstories/ boysschool.html; Internet; accessed 3 March 2008; Eagle Academy For Boys, Special To The Black Star News, January 30, 2008; Tanyanika Samuel, "Eagle Academy to get new complex," Daily News, December 19, 2007, tsamuels@nydaily news.com.

[277] The guiding principles upheld by the Academy curriculum and partners: Academic Excellence, Leadership, Character Development, Mentoring, Integrity and Community Service.

[278] Eagle was open with start-up grants from the Gates Foundation, the Carnegie Mellon Foundation and others. The classes are small; individual tutoring and attention are valued. It was one of two all-male schools to open in New York City in 2004.

[279] Elisabeth Hulette, "Single-sex Schools and Minority Achievement: Eagle Academy Takes on the 'Crisis' of Inner City Boys," http://www.coveringeducation.org/schoolstories/ boysschool.html; Internet; accessed 3 March 2008; "Single-sex education has gained popularity among public educators recently, in part thanks to new regulations released by the Bush

administration, first in 2002 under No Child Left Behind and then again in 2006, loosening Title IX's restrictions on single-sex schooling. Single-sex public schools had all but disappeared when Title IX was passed in 1972; now there are 10 in New York City and 51 nationwide."

[280] Peg Tyre, "The Trouble With Boys," *Newsweek*, January 30, 2006, 51.

[281] Special Programs: Boy's Club, Read Program, Boy Scouts, Council for Unity, New Jersey Nets Student Rewards Program; Extracurricular Activities: Chess Club, Debate Team, Martial Arts, Trumpet Academy, Poetry Club

[282] "Though they are much maligned by the public rhetoric as "super-predator" or the cause of "crime-being-out-of-control" and marched off to jail cells as a perverse solution to young black male existence, the threatening conditions of criminalization, death and disposability they face on a daily basis are not solely the gratuitous labor of their own hands."